Law Soup Media presents:

Do it Like a Boss

What Every Small Business Owner Needs to Know About Law and Taxes

Tristan Blaine, Esq.

Published by:
Law Soup Media

Copyright © 2022 by Tristan Blaine

Book design, illustrations by Tito Gonzalez

All rights reserved. No part of this book may be reproduced or transmitted in any form or by any means, without written permission from the publisher.

Law Soup Media is owned by Tristan Blaine. Law Soup and Law Soup Media are claimed trademarks of Tristan Blaine.

First trade paperback edition published 2022.

Printed in the United States of America, using paper not sourced from endangered old growth forests, forests of exceptional conservation value, or the Amazon Basin.

ISBN 979-8-218-00684-6

About the Author

Tristan Blaine founded Law Soup Media in 2014 and currently serves as its Editor-in-Chief. As a California-licensed lawyer, he helps people start and grow businesses of all kinds, with a focus on social enterprise (B Corps/benefit corporations).

Recognized as a leader in the community, he has been selected to the Super Lawyers list for several years. He volunteers with the Los Angeles LGBT Center, and has secured asylum for LGBT victims of persecution.

He received his bachelor's degree from UCLA, and obtained a law degree, with a concentration in Constitutional Law and Rights, from Cardozo Law School in New York City. Tristan enjoys meditation, yoga, and hiking in the mountains of Southern California.

About Law Soup Media

The Laws You Need to Know. In Edible Form.

Law Soup Media explains the law, simply. We tell you what you need to know about your legal rights and duties, civics and our government, and how it all works (or doesn't). This information empowers you to take charge of your life and to make a positive impact on society. Law Soup Media provides this content through a variety of media, including books, free web content, and a chatbot.

Law Soup Media's *Law is for Everyone* series

Law is Not for Lawyers (It's for Everyone):
 Empower Yourself with the Basics of Law and Civics

How to Be Free(lance):
 What Every Self-Employed Person Needs to Know About Law and Taxes

Do it Like a Boss:
 What Every Small Business Owner Needs to Know About Law and Taxes

Contents

1 - How to *Do it Like a Boss* 3

A Bit About Me 4
Practical Wisdom... 5
A Few Important Things to Note 7
How to Use this Book 10
What's in this Book.. 11

2 - Business: The Basics..15

What is a Business?... 15
Which Laws Apply to My Business?................................ 18
Magical Creations of Law... 19

3 - Small and New(born) Businesses....................23

Stages of Growth and Development 23
Small and Not-So-Small... 26
What is Considered a Startup?.. 27
Do Different Laws Apply to Small Businesses and Startups?.. 28

4 - Gimme Structure: Business Form and Structure 31

What Does it Mean to Be "Taxed As"?........................... 34
What is a Legal Entity (and What is Not an Entity)? 37
Why Form an Entity?... 41

Why Would You NOT Form, or Why Would You Wait to Form, an Entity? 46
Which Entity is Best? 47
How Do I Properly Set Up and Maintain My Business Structure? 60

5 - Business Taxes Are... Taxing 71

How Do Taxes Work for Small Business? 72
What Tax Treatment Should I Use? 79
OK so after I do all that, I'm done with taxes, right? 88
Is All This Worth It? 89
So How Do I Actually File My Taxes? 90
Taxes Recap 90

6 - Let Me See Your License and Registration 93

Do I Need to Register My Business? 93
Local Business License and Tax Filings 93
The ABCs of the DBA 94
Registering Your Professional or Business Activities 96
Regulation of Products 97
Seller's Permit 98
Registering as an Employer 99
Tax ID/EIN 99
Brick and Mortar Permits 99
Home-based Business 100

7 - Naming Names: Business Naming and Branding
.... 103

DBA.. 103

State Registration of Business 104

Trademark & Other Intellectual Property..................... 105

8 – Use Protection: Protecting Your Work........ 113

Protecting Tangible Work with Copyright 113

Protecting Ideas: Patent, Trade Secrets, and NDAs...... 121

9 – Working Well with Others (Contracts)........ 125

Contracts 101 126

What are the Main Types of Contracts for Small Business? 132

What are Common Types of Contract Clauses for Small Business?.. 133

How Contracts Work: Scenarios 140

10 – Get By with a Little Help from Your Workers 143

Freelancers vs. Employees... 144

Hiring Freelancers: A Guide 150

Hiring Employees: A Guide 151

11 – Launch Money.. 155

Bootstrapping.. 155

Loans 156

Equity Investment.. 157

Crowdfunding.. 159

12 - ... And Other Things Small Business Owners Should Know 163

Marketing and Advertising 163
Endorsements 164
Free Speech Isn't Free 164
Retail and Product-Related Issues................................ 165
Doing Business on the Internet 166

13 - When Things Go Wrong 169

Help! I Didn't Get Paid! 169
Help! My Client or Customer is Suing (or Threatening to Sue) Me!.. 172

14 - Helping Hands: Getting Legal and Tax Help for Small Business 175

Hiring Lawyers and CPAs... 175
Legal Costs 177
Should I use LegalZoom or other document preparation services?... 179

15 - What Comes Next? 183

Acknowledgments 185

Legalese Translator (Glossary)..........................186
Worksheet for Small Business...........................191

How to *Do it Like a Boss*

"And the day came when the risk to remain tight in a bud was more painful than the risk it took to blossom."

- Anaïs Nin

1 – How to *Do it Like a Boss*

So, you want to run your own business? **Why**? Seriously, take a minute to write down your reasons here:

_____

_____

_____

When things get tough, when you're overwhelmed, or when you don't want to have to read about legal and tax stuff anymore, come back to these reasons. If the reasons are compelling enough, they will give you the mental boost you need to keep the business going.

As a small business owner myself (my law practice and Law Soup Media), I can tell you what my "Why" is: I wanted to do something very different than what I had done in the past. It's kind of a negative motivation, but it definitely works. I saw this on the cap of a bottle of iced tea once: "Finding myself by process of elimination." It immediately resonated with me, and in fact, I still have that cap, and I'm looking at it right now.

I've tried many things in my career. I would rather not get into specifics (well, maybe if you buy me a drink or two). Let's just say, these roles were not for me. So I decided to try becoming an entrepreneur.

You may find this surprising, but I'm not naturally a business-oriented person. It was only later in life when I realized that, in order to further my goals, I had to turn myself into a business person. To my own surprise, I found the business mindset to be quite a good fit for me. I love thinking about how to provide services and products that can improve people's lives. And I wanted to help others do the same. It's this motivation that keeps me going during the challenging times.

Finding your motivation is ~~probably~~ absolutely the most important part of being a small business owner. Once you have that, the rest is.... well...doable. But don't presume that I'm hereby giving you permission to run your own business. That would actually be quite arrogant of me, wouldn't it? You don't need my permission, of course. One of the great things about operating your own business is that you don't need anyone's permission to do so. Well, except that the government won't let you carry out illegal business activities. So, there's that.

You will face many challenges, including figuring out the relevant laws, sorting out administrative issues, or acquiring and maintaining clients and customers. As for the legal requirements and best practices, this book will help with that. And believe it or not, there are lawyers out there that are happy to assist with small business issues, and at a reasonable cost. OK, maybe not many, but they're there. I'm here. And I'm here to help.

A Bit About Me

In 2009, full of optimism and idealism, I went to law school to work towards that great promise of "liberty and justice for all." Yes, really! I received a concentration in constitutional law and rights, ready to make the world a little more fair for everyone. I figured most other lawyers were interested in the same. But I soon became disillusioned. After graduating and working for other lawyers, I realized there were not enough lawyers dedicated to providing high-quality legal services at reasonable rates.

So, in 2014 I started my own law practice to make legal services more accessible to small businesses. I focus on advising and teaching people how to make the law work for them, explaining it in a way that normal people can understand. I also believe in using simple, reasonable, transparent pricing. Unfortunately, this approach is all too rare. But it's the right thing to do.

Around the same time that I started my law practice, I also created Law Soup Media to provide free and low-cost legal information to the public about many areas of the law – from consumer issues, to employment, tenants rights, civil rights, and yes, small business law. It started with a website, LawSoup.org, and now we have published these Law Soup Media books. By purchasing the books, you are not only helping yourself, but you are helping us provide free online information, so thank you for that.

Practical Wisdom

In my time working with small businesses, I have seen my clients make many mistakes. I have a bit of practical wisdom to help you avoid these. Throughout your entrepreneurial journey, you will face some difficult choices. Should you always strictly follow the best legal and business practices? Or can you let things slide sometimes, maybe to build goodwill with a customer or client?

It's really about your risk tolerance. When making business decisions about things like whether to take on a particular client, or whether to bring on a partner, keep in mind that there are always risks involved. *Risky Business* is not just a movie from the '80s. The good news is that there are many ways to build a safety net, and I will discuss these. While nothing is bulletproof, if you stick with the best practices, you will minimize your risk of legal issues.

Let's try a thought experiment. Try to imagine how you will feel if, after making your decision, things go poorly. It may not be a fun exercise, but it can save you from unnecessary suffering. For example, say you weren't sure whether to take on a client who declines to pay your standard 50% upfront deposit. Their policy is to pay nothing until the work is complete. You are uneasy with this, but perhaps you don't have many other clients at the moment and you are feeling somewhat desperate. You think to yourself: the client wouldn't refuse to pay, especially after they see the great work I do for them, right? So you do your work diligently over the course of several weeks, and the client seems quite pleased with the result. You then send them a bill for $10,000, as agreed, and what is the response? Radio silence.

Yes, it's terrible, but this kind of thing happens all. the. time. And unfortunately there is no quick and easy legal fix for it. So, how would you feel if this happened to you? Now, considering this possible outcome, would you take the client or not? Exercise over. Here's your first **hot tip** of the book:

> **HOT TIP:** Be good to your future self! It's important to acknowledge the risks and understand the potential consequences of any major action. Then consider what you can do to minimize the risks. If you can get this down to a level that is acceptable to you, then maybe that's the right decision for you.

A Few Important Things to Note

This information applies throughout the U.S.

Laws in the U.S. related to business are made at the federal, state, and local levels. I will mostly refer to federal law and nationally applicable concepts, but I also provide examples of state and local laws. So, the information referenced here is generally applicable to businesses based anywhere in the United States. For your state and local laws, check the Law Soup website and reach out to local lawyers.

Exceptions to the rule

A law or legal principle that seems simple and straightforward may not always hold true in every situation. There are almost always exceptions to a rule. Life is messy, so law is messy. When explaining a law or concept, I try to use terms like "generally" or "in general" to indicate that there are or may be exceptions. You will see these words frequently throughout. Even when I don't use these terms, keep in mind there are always exceptions, except when there aren't. Just accept it.

Gray areas

Related to the concept of exceptions to the rule is the idea that the law is filled with gray areas. (Or is it *grey* areas? This is its own gray area!). While many legal rules or principles are firmly settled and generally free from doubt or dispute (known as **black letter law**), others may be ambiguous or in flux. I do my best to let you know how solid a rule is or isn't.

Even when a rule is settled, it may be a gray area as to whether the facts support a finding one way or another. An example is the requirement that a party to a contract must clearly indicate their agreement to that contract. What counts as indicating agreement may be up for interpretation. How about if you propose a deal, and the other person responds "looks good," or simply "OK"? Did that person definitely agree to the terms of the contract, or were they merely acknowledging that they received it or reviewed it? Ultimately, this may need to be decided by a judge or jury.

Everything changes

As with life, the law changes all the time, so some of the information here may be out of date at some point. Check the Law Soup website and discuss with a lawyer to make sure you have the latest info.

This is not legal advice (and a book can never tell you everything you need to know about the law)

Reading this book does not mean you can necessarily handle your own legal issues. It does not take the place of *actual* legal advice from an *actual* lawyer who can tell you how the law applies to your particular situation. Nothing in here is meant to be legal *advice*. Rather, it's general legal *information*. Because of the gray areas, exceptions to the rules, and often-changing laws that we just discussed, figuring out the right course of action on a legal question or problem can be tricky for lawyers, let alone non-lawyers.

Of course, you should be able to handle many tasks and decisions on your own, even when there are legal implications involved. You can't rely on lawyers for everything. But beware the Dunning-Kruger effect, which is when a person learns the basics on a topic, and then overestimates their level of knowledge. This often leads them to make mistakes without realizing it.

So, how do you know what you don't know? Ask a lawyer! A good one will tell you when you need them and when you don't. You will almost certainly need a lawyer from time to time, and I will emphasize this at various times throughout (maybe too often!). The information here can help you be more confident and efficient in consulting with lawyers about your issues and concerns. It will save you money and time (and time is money so you'll save *lots* of money).

Nobody's perfect

Even with significant research and fact-checking, mistakes and inaccuracies are inevitable. Please help us and everyone else by letting us know if you think you see an error!

How to Use this Book

Do it Like a Boss is the third book of the *Law is for Everyone* series. Before reading this one, be sure to read the first, *Law is Not for Lawyers (It's for Everyone)*, for the basics of the legal system. This book builds off that one, and I reference it from time to time.

You may be tempted to skip over some parts of *Do it Like a Boss* which do not seem relevant to you at this particular time in your small business journey. But the best way to benefit from the book is to read it in its entirety once through, and then re-read the parts you have questions about. Because the various parts of law are interconnected, it starts to make much more sense when you learn how all the pieces fit together.

Secondly, you need to know the basics of business law *before* you have any issues, so that when an emergency or surprising event comes up, you won't worry so much because you will have a sense of how serious or not serious it is. And you will have a general idea how to start dealing with it. After you've read the book once, and later you have a question that you have forgotten the answer to, you can then come back and re-read the relevant section.

This book is designed to help you proactively work through the legal aspects of operating a business. As you read, I encourage you to make notes in the book, and you can also use the Notes pages at the end. Also towards the end of the book is a worksheet with a checklist to help you get a sense of which steps you have completed and what you still need to do. It's all a process, so if you feel overwhelmed, just take it one step at a time!

What's in this Book

Small business owners, like everyone else, need to know the basics of the legal system, which you should read about in *Law is Not for Lawyers (It's for Everyone)*. Concepts like jurisdiction and the hierarchy of laws are essential for small businesses to know about. Laws affecting businesses are made at the federal, state, and local levels, so it's important to know which applies to you and when.

Once you have the legal basics covered, as a small business owner you need to know about the following areas of law, which we will discuss. These include general business basics (Chapter 2); the basic concepts for small and new businesses in particular (Chapter 3); how to structure and organize your business (Chapter 4); business taxes (Chapter 5); licenses, permits, and other regulations (Chapter 6);

naming and branding your business, trademark, etc. (Chapter 7); protecting your work and work product, copyright, patent, trade secret, etc. (Chapter 8); best practices for working with and for others, using contracts (Chapter 9); hiring a workforce, and employment law (Chapter 10); funding your business (Chapter 11); other miscellaneous things for business owners (Chapter 12); what to do when things go wrong, and how to resolve disputes (Chapter 13); and how small business owners can get affordable legal help (Chapter 14).

"Opportunities are usually disguised as hard work, so most people don't recognize them."

— Ann Landers

2 - Business: The Basics

What is a Business?

Business and not-business

When one or more people regularly provide a service or product in order to earn profits, this is a business. This broad definition encompasses much human activity. On one end of the spectrum, charging people to walk their dogs is a business. On the other end, designing and selling millions of smartphones is also a business.

What is not a business?

As you can see from the simple definition above, there are three essential aspects to any business: 1) providing a product or service to others, 2) making a profit, and 3) doing so on an ongoing basis. If you have the first part but not the second, you either have a hobby or a non-profit. If you have the second part but not the first, you are either the recipient of a generous donor, or you are running a scam! If you don't have the third part, this is just a one-off (or maybe two-off, etc) transaction.

A so-called "hobby business" is one which makes little, if any, money, even after several years. The IRS does not allow a business to be claimed as a loss on a tax return unless it is a legitimate profit-motivated business. The "3-of-5" test says that if a business makes a profit in at least 3 out of 5 consecutive years, it is presumed to have a legitimate profit motive. If not, you would have to prove the legitimacy of the business through other means, such as accounting records, business registrations, and/or advertising.

As is obvious from the name, a non-profit organization is not a business. However, a non-profit can certainly sell goods or services, although there are various rules and regulations on non-profits engaging in these practices. A non-profit also may (and should) use basic financial practices including creating and sticking to a budget, and using resources efficiently.

Businesses come in all shapes and sizes

Like the human body, or some kind of shape-shifting alien, a business can take many forms. It can be as small as a sole owner-operator, or as large as millions of owners and employees. But bigger is not necessarily always better.

If you operate a business as a sole owner, this certainly simplifies things quite a bit. You do not need to worry about figuring out how decisions will be made (unless you have multiple personalities in your head). On the other hand, you are solely responsible for, well, everything. This can work just fine for certain types of businesses. A sole owner of a business that provides a personal service is essentially a freelancer, which is generally an operation that is manageable for one person. For in-depth legal and other information on freelancing, check out Law Soup Media's

How to Be Free(lance): What Every Self-Employed Person Needs to Know About Law and Taxes.

If your business model is more complicated, you may consider partnering with at least one other person. Of course, there are pros and cons to getting more people on board. Bad news first: more partners means more potential disagreements and conflicts, and more ways the pie is sliced. The good news is that you may be able to grow a larger pie (suddenly I'm in the mood to go to a bakery). Each additional owner can bring capital (money), expertise, their network, and even emotional support.

Businesses can also vary significantly in terms of time and space (and spacetime, but I'm not a physicist so I'll leave that one alone). Some people think it's not a "real" business if it's just a side-hustle that you do in your spare time, or if you don't have a separate physical location to operate it. This is not true. Remember our definition above? As long as you do something on an ongoing basis (perhaps at least a few hours per month), and you are aiming to earn a profit from it, it's a business.

> **HOT TIP:** Don't worry about trying to fit some conventional idea of what a business should look like. Your business can be successful however you define success.

Which Laws Apply to My Business?

Various federal, state, and local laws and taxes apply to businesses, so you will need to know about all of these which are relevant to your jurisdiction(s) (location(s)). State and local laws and taxes apply based on where the business operates. Depending on your situation, business locations can be defined as where the business owners live, where the employees work, and/or where the customers are. As far as personal income taxes, the state where the business owners live generally taxes the owners based on their business earnings. We'll discuss taxes in Chapter 5.

If you have a home-based business, this can simplify things (or complicate things if the business operation competes for space with family members!). The city and state you live in would generally be the relevant jurisdictions for determining the regulations and taxes that apply. But not all businesses can be based out of a home, as this may violate local zoning laws. See Chapter 6.

For business owners who do most or all their work on a laptop and online, it may be hard to know exactly where you are considered to be doing business. Say you have an online-only Etsy shop. Or perhaps you just do drop-shipping, where you don't even handle the inventory at all. The general rule is this: unless you operate from a physical location outside your home, such as an office, coworking space, or store, your business is deemed to be based out of your home.

If you have a single business location outside your home, the business is subject to the laws and taxes of that city and state. If you have multiple business locations, you would designate one as the "headquarters" for certain things like incorporating. Each additional location is also subject to its location's local laws, such as zoning.

For most small businesses and small business owners, jurisdiction issues are quite straightforward. But if you think you have a complicated situation, you should discuss with an accountant for tax purposes, and a lawyer for complying with regulations.

Magical Creations of Law

Many legal processes involve a relatively straightforward filing of paperwork. Some examples include forming a corporation, or obtaining a business license, both of which require you to file a piece of paper with the government.

However, a counterintuitive concept that comes up sometimes, particularly in business law, is that some things are created without any paperwork at all. Certain types of business structures, contracts, and copyright and trademark rights are created "automatically," or by **operation of law** based on certain actions you take.

These creations of law are kind of like magic. You know when you wave your wand and say an incantation in Latin, and an inanimate object comes to life? It's kind of like that, without all the smoke. But be careful with your powers, as you can make things happen without even realizing it!

Say you want to create a work of art. The second you put the paint on the canvas, then – POOF! – you automatically own the copyright for that work. You don't get any kind of certificate or anything. It is simply understood and accepted by the law and the courts that you now own it. Of course, you can also fill out an application and get a copyright registration certificate, but that is "next-level," as we'll discuss in Chapter 8.

Or say you offer to pay someone to create a website for your business. They agree to it, but then you realize you don't have the money to pay for that right now. You may think you can just politely back out because you didn't sign anything, but not so fast. With your words alone, even without specifically intending it, you may indeed have created a legally binding contract.

We will discuss this concept of operation of law a few times throughout the book, so hopefully you will get a good understanding of how it works.

> "There's no shortage of remarkable ideas, what's missing is the will to execute them."
>
> – Seth Godin

3 - Small and New(born) Businesses

Like humans, businesses start off as small, shiny new things. When you are new to the world, there is much to do and figure out. But it gets easier once you get past the growing pains. Let's talk about the early stages in the life of a business.

Stages of Growth and Development

For the best chance of a thriving business, while minimizing costs and risks, there is a suggested order of operations to follow. Although you may get very excited at the prospect of your business idea becoming a full-fledged business, I would caution against jumping in and starting any legal processes such as incorporating and trademarking just yet. In business, you must maintain a sense of practicality. If things don't work out as planned, you don't want to have wasted too much money or efforts.

On the other hand, there may be certain deadlines to meet. In many cities and states, there is a requirement to secure a business license or permit within a certain number of days after "starting" business. When have you officially started your business? Usually it's when you have made your first sale, but this can vary by jurisdiction.

You may also want the protections and benefits of a proper business entity before you get too many customers or clients. And you may want to secure and protect your business name as soon as possible to ensure that others don't start using it first. You must weigh these competing considerations when determining the right time to take the steps towards formalizing your business.

> **HOT TIP:** A good time to start setting up a formal business structure and other legal related tasks is the moment when the business starts to gain traction, with at least a few regular customers or clients.

The idea phase

A typical business starts at conception – of an idea. If you think you have an amazing idea that will change the world and that could bring you great fortune, don't be afraid to share it with others. Many would-be entrepreneurs jealously guard their business ideas because they think someone is going to steal them and start the business before they get a chance. It could happen, certainly, but much of the success of a business is due to great *execution* of the idea. Based on your unique combination of skills and experience, you may be one of the few people who can properly implement the business.

At this point, you probably don't need to worry so much about ensuring people sign confidentiality agreements,

NDAs, and such. That said, if you have developed a highly technical invention, you may indeed want to keep the details of it locked up, and possibly get a patent. See more about protecting business ideas in Chapter 8.

The plan phase

To turn your idea into a real-life business, it's highly recommended to have a plan for how the business could work. Notice I'm avoiding the term "Business Plan," because it often conjures up an image of a 100-page report full of market research, with charts and graphs galore. This is usually unnecessary, and just the thought of it can hold you back from diving in and getting the business going.

Most entrepreneurs don't even have the time or resources to create this kind of document. If you are able to do it, and need to for a particular reason – a financier is asking for one, for example – then by all means, get to it. But for the most part, if you can fill a page with the basics about potential revenue and costs, branding and marketing, and funding, that may be good enough to get started on the right foot.

The testing phase

After you have worked out most of the details of the business (at least on paper), you should start by testing the waters to see if the idea has legs. Talk to friends, family, and colleagues to see what they think about it. If possible, try offering your proposed product or service on a small scale to see if people are willing to pay for it, and how much.

If you get some traction, you may be ready to take the next steps towards launching. Otherwise, you may want to go back to the idea or plan phases.

The launch phase

You have ideated, planned, and tested, and now you are ready to send your business out into the world. If the business requires a significant amount of money to launch, you would want to start looking into options for funding (see Chapter 11). Make sure to take care of all the legal stuff at this point (see Chapters 4, 5, 6... basically the rest of the book).

Keep in mind that, to be successful, a business must continually evolve. You may find yourself going back to the early stages of ideating, planning and testing. Significant changes in the business may require revising your business structure, permits, etc. It's all a process!

Where are you in this process? Is it time to get your ducks in a row, or are you not quite ready for that yet? Feel free to make some notes: _____

_____

_____

Small and Not-So-Small

What defines a *small* business? There is no single definition. A business is generally "sized up" in terms of a few factors: number of owners, number of employees, and revenue/profit.

When most people think of a "small business," it's usually a company owned by one person or a few people, with maybe a few employees. However, the U.S. Small Business Administration defines small business in a very counterintuitive way. Depending on the industry, the SBA's definition of small business can include companies with up to 1,500 employees or $40 million in revenue![1] One of the SBA's goals is to make sure *smaller* businesses have a chance at government contracts, and that the biggest fish don't swallow up everything. So, when the SBA defines small business, it basically means NOT the Amazons or Walmarts, which have billions in revenue and millions of employees.

That said, for most legal purposes, the size of a business isn't that important. Most business laws and principles apply just the same to small business and very large corporations. So, yes, when you are "getting down to business," size matters, but it's not as important as some think it is.

What is Considered a Startup?

There is also no strict definition of the term "startup." But In the popular discourse, the term "startup" has come to refer to a business that is just starting out, but expects to "scale up" and grow quite fast to become a large company.

If you consider your business a "startup" in this sense, and want to grow very quickly, you will probably take some different legal steps than with a traditional small business. In particular, if you are hoping to get major investment, such as from a venture capital (VC) fund, this would affect what type of legal structure makes the most sense. We will discuss business structures later on.

Do Different Laws Apply to Small Businesses and Startups?

Most laws apply to small businesses and startups the same as to large, established businesses. One exception is employment laws, many of which only apply to businesses with a certain number of employees. For example, some state antidiscrimination laws apply only to employers with 5 or more employees. Additionally, the Affordable Care Act's requirement that employers provide health insurance for employees applies to companies with at least 50 employees.

Some industry-specific laws apply differently based on the size of a business, such as more regulations that apply to large banks but not small banks. Other than that, most laws, rules and regulations are much the same for small and large companies alike, including business structures, business names, intellectual property, consumer rights, and more.

"Many of life's failures are people who did not realize how close they were to success when they gave up."

- Thomas Edison

4 – Gimme Structure: Business Form and Structure

One of the most important aspects of business law is the form or structure under which you operate. I'm not talking about bricks or steel here. Of course, physical structure is important too, but I'm not an architect (I've always thought it would be fun though).

A business structure consists of two separate and distinct parts: (1) **legal structure**; and (2) **tax treatment** (also sometimes referred to as *tax structure* or *tax classification*, but I will stick with *tax treatment* for clarity). Legal structure is how a business is set up under the law, whereas a tax treatment is how the business is set up under the tax system.

It's very important to understand this distinction, but, I'll be honest, it can be quite confusing. The bewilderment mostly lies in the fact that there is some overlap in the terms used for legal structures and tax treatments (hey, I don't make the rules, I'm just the messenger). A **sole proprietorship** refers to a type of *legal structure*, as well as a type of *tax treatment*. This is also true of a **general partnership**. A **corporation** is a legal structure, while a **C corporation** and an **S corporation** are types of tax treatments.

To keep things clear, I will use superscripts to indicate when I am referring to a legal structure (sole proprietorship^L) or a tax treatment (sole proprietorship^T). When I use the term

corporation on its own, I am only referring to a type of legal structure, while **C corporation** and **S corporation** only refer to tax treatments, not legal structures.

There are four legal structures that small business owners should be aware of. These can be split into non-entities or quasi-entities which are not legally separate from the owner(s), and formal entities which have their own legal existence.

Quasi-entities or Non-entities:

1. Sole Proprietorship^L
2. General Partnership^L

Formal entities:

3. LLC
4. Corporation

As for tax treatments, there are also four that small businesses should be familiar with:

1. Sole Proprietorship^T
2. General Partnership^T
3. S corporation
4. C corporation

Now let's put it all together. For the legal structures of sole proprietorships and general partnerships, the tax treatments are straightforward. A sole proprietorship^L can only be taxed as a sole proprietorship^T, and a general partnership^L is taxed as a general partnership^T.

Legal structures and tax treatments – one owner

Legal structure	Can be taxed as...
Sole proprietorship[L]	Sole proprietorship[T]
LLC	Sole proprietorship[T] C Corporation S Corporation
Corporation	C Corporation S Corporation

Legal structures and tax treatments – multiple owners

Legal structure	Can be taxed as...
General partnership[L]	General partnership[T]
LLC	General partnership[T] C Corporation S Corporation
Corporation	C Corporation S Corporation

Where things get complicated (in a good way) is that with certain legal structures, you can choose among various tax treatments in order to pay the lowest amount in taxes. This is called a "check the box" election. A corporation can be taxed as a C corporation or as an S corporation. An LLC can be taxed as a sole proprietorship[T] (if one owner), a general partnership[T] (if more than one owner), or as an S corporation or C corporation (regardless of how many owners). Note that an LLC is only a legal structure, never a tax treatment.

What Does it Mean to Be "Taxed As"?

The concept of a business being "taxed as" a certain tax treatment is how it is treated by the IRS and state tax agencies. The taxman and taxwoman generally don't care about your legal structure (although they will ask about it), they just want to know about your tax treatment. In contrast, the state business registration agencies (particularly your state's **Secretary of State**) don't really care about your tax treatment, just your legal structure.

So, if you are an LLC, taxed as an S corporation, the Secretary of State sees that you are an LLC; the IRS sees that you are an S corporation. It's like cosplay: when you wear a Batman costume, normal people see you as yourself dressed up as Batman. But the IRS acts like you really are Batman! The following diagrams show the process of selecting an entity and tax treatment.

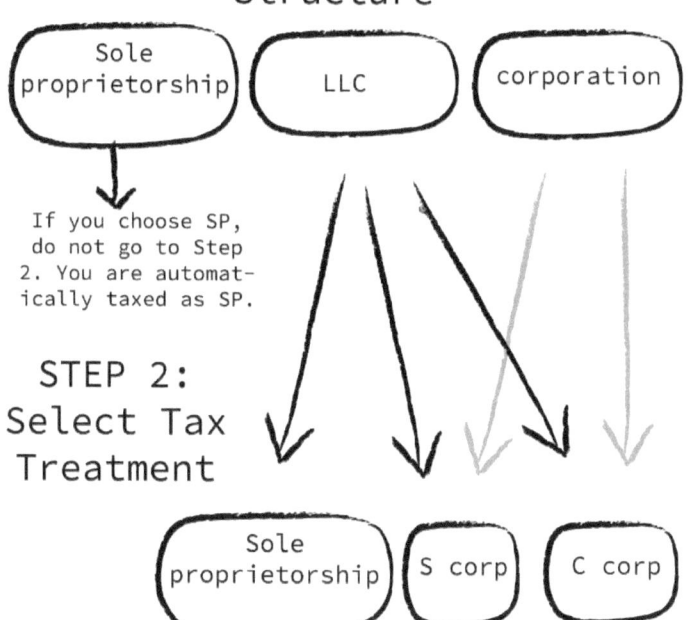

Do it Like a Boss

Process of Creating Legal Structure + Tax Treatment (Multiple Business Owners)

STEP 1: Create Legal Structure

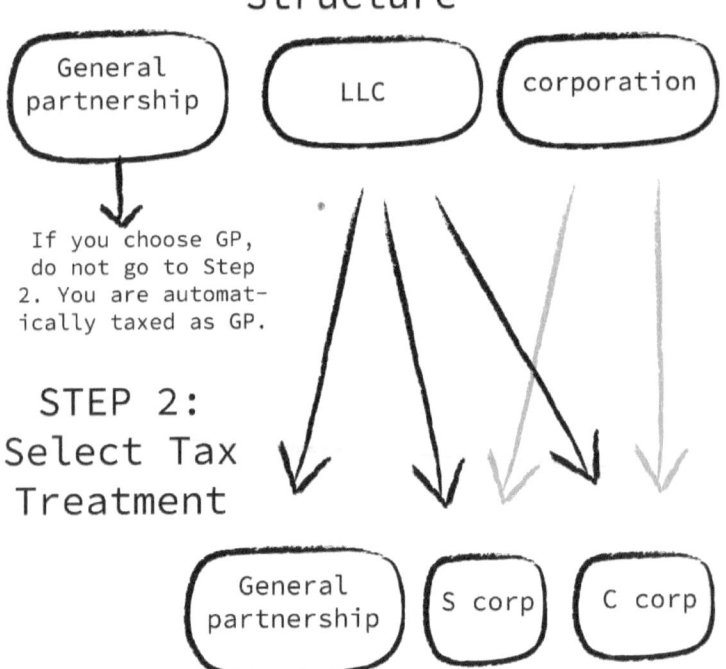

If you choose GP, do not go to Step 2. You are automatically taxed as GP.

STEP 2: Select Tax Treatment

What is a Legal Entity (and What is Not an Entity)?

To grasp the concept of a legal entity, it's helpful to start with some examples of what are NOT legal entities, including sole proprietorships, general partnerships, DBAs, etc.

Sole proprietorship

If you are the sole owner of a business, and you haven't formed an entity (usually an LLC or corporation) for the business, by definition you are a sole proprietorship. As soon as you start performing any kind of services for money, by the magic of the **operation of law**, you are a sole proprietor, and you operate a sole proprietorship^L (congratulations!). You don't *form* a sole proprietorship^L, you just *are* one.

In a sole proprietorship^L, you are the business and the business is you. While there isn't anything to do to form the sole proprietorship^L, there are various requirements to fulfill which apply to any business form. We will discuss these requirements in Chapter 6.

General partnership

If you co-own a business with at least one other person, and you haven't created a formal entity like an LLC or corporation for the business, you are "automagically" a general partnership. You may indeed have this form of business whether you like it or not, and whether you even know it or not. That's right, unless you specify otherwise, by

operation of law, a general partnership is created when two or more people work together intending to earn profits. In a general partnership, each person can be held legally responsible for anything the other people do in the working relationship. And the others may have a claim to profits that you didn't even anticipate. A few years down the road, when you are making your millions, those initial collaborators may come knocking, seeking their piece of the pie (mmm....pie).

Maybe you thought your friend was just helping you out, as a favor. Perhaps you even compensated them well. Or maybe you thought you were hiring someone as an employee or independent contractor. You never considered that these people could claim any ownership in *your* business!

If you want to avoid all this, first, be careful in how you discuss the business with others who will work with you. Avoid phrases like "let's partner up on this." If you feel that it's your business, instead say something like "do you want to do some work for my business?" Have them sign a contract that includes a provision that you are not operating as a partnership. (A contract is like a condom – never get down to business with others without one!)

This contract should clearly describe what they will do for the business, what the compensation will be, and that they are not entitled to any ownership or share of the profits. You would generally either define it in the contract as an independent contractor or employment relationship.

On the other hand, if you *do* intend to operate as a partnership, you will also need a contract (of course). In partnerships, if you haven't entered into a **partnership agreement** that specifies how profits and losses will be split among the partners, then, by operation of law, all profits and losses are split equally, regardless of how much money or effort each partner puts in. Don't like that? Make sure everyone signs a partnership agreement! See more on this below, in the section Slicing Up the Pie (more pie!). All that said, if it's an ongoing collaborative situation, it's probably better to set up a formal entity (e.g. LLC or corporation) instead, as we'll discuss.

The general partnership is not a formal entity, but more of a quasi-entity. A partnership can take certain actions as if it were a separate entity, including holding property and entering into contracts. However, a partnership always acts on behalf of the partners. In contrast, a legal entity acts on behalf of itself (directed by its leadership, of course). Also, a partnership structure is somewhat ephemeral, as it generally dissolves if one of the partners leaves. In contrast, an LLC or corporation is presumed to be perpetual until it is dissolved.

Other things that are not entities
DBA

People sometimes say their business "is" a DBA, but this is not correct. A DBA is NOT a business structure; it is merely a required filing for some businesses.

DBA stands for "Doing Business As." As in, for example, you are Jane Goodall *doing business as* Monkeying Around Productions. In this case, you may need to file the proper paperwork for the DBA. See Chapter 6 for more on DBAs.

S Corporation/C Corporation

As discussed, an S Corporation or C Corporation are types of tax treatments that can be *applied to* a legal structure. They are not their own legal structure. See Chapter 5 for more on S Corporations and C Corporations.

Business license

A business license from your city or state is not an entity and does not create an entity. It is simply a filing that many businesses in certain cities and/or states are required to do. See Chapter 6 for more on this.

Entities: a life of their own

Unlike sole proprietorships and general partnerships, LLCs and corporations have a life of their own. For example, when you form an LLC, the LLC exists separate from you. Even though you may have complete control over it, it's still a separate entity. It's like having your own robot, except the LLC has no possibility of becoming self-aware and turning against you. The law even considers business entities as separate "persons," with their own legal rights and responsibilities. For example, a corporation or LLC can be found guilty of a crime! Obviously you can't put a corporation behind bars, but they can face significant fines of millions of dollars.

When you create an LLC or corporation for a business that is a sole proprietorship or partnership, this takes the place of the sole proprietorship or partnership. To set up formal entities including an LLC or corporation, you must file paperwork with the state government agency that registers companies. In most states this agency is called the **Secretary of State** (not to be confused with the U.S. Secretary of State, which handles foreign affairs) or Secretary of the Commonwealth.

Why Form an Entity?

LLCs and corporations have developed a kind of mythological status, as if they are the 8th world wonder. While the advantages of these entities are often overhyped, they can be quite powerful in the right hands. How do you know if your business should have one of these structures? Call your doctor to find out if these treatments are right for you.

More seriously, the following two chapters will help you understand the pros and cons of forming an entity. But you should also talk to a lawyer and tax professional regarding your situation.

In determining whether to form an entity or not, you should start with the following 2-step process:

Step 1: Will an entity help me save on taxes?

If yes, then it's a no-brainer! Put this book down and proceed directly to setting up your entity. But wait, how do you know if an entity will reduce your tax bill? This may start to get annoying, but really, a tax professional will help you know for sure. For now, here's a very basic and over-generalized test: if your business is consistently making good profits (say, over $100K), then perhaps you could possibly lower your taxes with an entity.

If you have determined that an entity will not help you save on taxes, go to step 2.

Step 2: Is an entity worth it to me for its other benefits?

Well, what are the benefits, exactly? Other than potentially saving on taxes, which we discussed, there are at least four good reasons to form an entity: protect your personal assets; organize business finances and other administrative tasks; enhance business credibility and marketing; and make it easier to sell the business if you wanted to do so at some point.

Benefit #1: Taxes

As I alluded to, you may be able to save some serious money in taxes by forming an entity. Chapter 5 has all the deets.

Benefit #2: Personal asset protection ("limited liability")

Other than taxes, the "superpower" that an LLC or corporation provides business owners is protecting personal assets, aka **limited liability**. This means that the entity acts to shield the personal assets of the owners from the obligations of the business, such as debts or lawsuits.

What does this mean in practical terms? Let's say a customer has a problem with a product you sold them, and they want to sue. If your business is structured as an LLC, the customer would generally only be able to sue the LLC, not you as the business owner. So, even if the customer obtains a $1 million judgment against the business (ouch), only the LLC's bank accounts or other property can be used to satisfy the judgment. The LLC "quarantines" these problems to keep them inside the "house" of the LLC, so they don't spread. Your personal bank accounts, car, home, or prized Pokémon card collection would generally be safe from the contagion.

As a conscientious business owner who would not want to evade your responsibilities, why should you care about limited liability? Even when run properly, a business can face significant, unanticipated problems. Sometimes a product can cause unknown harms to consumers, even after extensive safety testing. And sudden changes in consumer trends and demands can tank any successful business, leaving it unable to pay its debts.

A quick history lesson: the concept of limited liability gained traction in the early 1800s to incentivize entrepreneurs to take risks and start businesses. Many scholars believe that this protection was a major factor in the unprecedented growth of Western economies, the creation of the modern capitalist system, and in particular, the global dominance of the United States. The superpower of limited liability may have led to the U.S. becoming its own superpower. And you can get access to this power by simply filing some documents!

Certainly, even limited liability has its limits. Actions taken on behalf of a business that directly harm others can subject owners and officers to criminal penalties, including fines and jail time. Still, these cases are often hard to prove. More common holes in the armor occur when a business does not follow proper procedures (which we will discuss) and thus loses its liability shield. As long as you remain conscientious and diligent with your business responsibilities, you can maintain your legal protection, not to mention your integrity.

A particular concern for small business owners is that many banks, commercial landlords, and others require the owners of an entity to *personally guarantee* or co-sign the obligation. As to these parties, you would not have the benefits of limited liability, and your personal assets could be on the hook.

You can (and should) also protect the business's assets by obtaining business insurance. This comes in various forms, such as a kind of blanket policy usually known as **commercial general liability** (CGL) insurance, or **property liability** insurance, or **errors and omissions** (E&O) for certain licensed professionals. Talk to an insurance broker for details.

Benefit #3: Organize finances and other administrative tasks

Having a separate entity helps to separate business finances and property from personal finances and property. While you can maintain this separation as a sole proprietor or partnership through careful planning, the structure and formalities of an entity make it much easier to do so. It also makes this distinction clear to the outside world.

Benefit #4: Credibility and marketing

Customers, clients, vendors, and banks tend to have more respect for, or may even require you to be, an LLC or corporation rather than a sole proprietor or partnership.

Benefit #5: Easier to sell the business

Over time, you may develop value in your business, particularly in your brand. If your brand has taken on a life of its own, at some point you may want to cash out and have someone else take it over. If the business is set up as an LLC or corporation, then a buyer would simply purchase the entity, which should contain all the business assets and branding.

Why Would You NOT Form, or Why Would You Wait to Form, an Entity?

Two reasons: expense and paperwork. In most states the filing fee for an entity is around $100, but it can be as high as $500 (Massachusetts). And most states have a minimum annual tax or fee on the entity, regardless of income. This is also an average of about $100, but can be as high as $800 per year (California). The lowest cost states (as of this writing) are Arizona, New Mexico, and Mississippi, all of which have a filing fee of $50, and $0 minimum fee or tax per year.

But before you start filling out the paperwork for an Arizona LLC, you better be prepared to move there. You can't avoid your own state's fees and taxes by setting up an entity in another state. See "Can I Save Money on Taxes and Fees by Forming My Entity in a Different State?" below.

Another drawback is that you need to follow formalities for the entity, including preparing paperwork, keeping detailed business records of income, expenses, etc. That said, you should do these things anyway, as they are just good business practices.

Even with the expenses and paperwork, having an entity is almost certainly worth it. As we will discuss, you could end up saving much more in taxes than you pay in costs.

Bottom line: don't let fees and paperwork deter you from (properly) setting up an entity. If you have consistent and substantial earnings, it's probably time to get everything in place to start developing good practices, and for the peace of mind (priceless!).

Which Entity is Best?

Once you've decided to go for it and set up an entity, the next question is, well, which one? Most small businesses can usually narrow it down right away to two options: an LLC or a corporation.

There are other types of entities, but they are not as common, and not appropriate for most businesses. I will not focus on these, but for your reference, there are at least two other types of entities that you may come across: the **limited partnership (LP)**, and the **limited liability partnership (LLP)** (Note: while there are various types of partnerships, the term "partnership" on its own is usually used to refer to a general partnership).

A limited partnership is similar to a general partnership, except that one of the partners is a passive investor rather than an active participant in the business. An LLP is usually used for certain licensed professions including accountants, architects, and lawyers. Even if you have a passive investor, or are a licensed professional, a corporation or LLC still may be a better option; but talk to a lawyer and tax professional to be sure.

Despite the alternative forms of entities, the real action is in LLCs and corporations. and following is an explanation of these.

Corporation

A corporation has a somewhat complicated structure, at least on paper, and generally involves a bit more paperwork than an LLC. To create a corporation, you file a document or form, usually called the **articles of incorporation**, with your state's secretary of state. This founding document, which is like the "constitution" of the corporation, is actually relatively simple, in which you list some basic characteristics for the corporation. At a minimum, it usually must include the corporation's name, address, total number of shares the corporation may issue, and **agent for service of process**.

That last one might sound scary, like Agent Smith from *The Matrix*, but it's really not. Also known as a **registered agent**, or something similar, the agent for service of process is simply the person responsible for receiving the papers if the corporation is ever sued. You see, if someone wants to sue your corporation (which hopefully won't happen), they need to physically hand the summons document to a person who represents the company (they *serve* the *agent* of the company with the *process* of starting a lawsuit). Depending on the state, this person usually can be anyone associated with the company, including yourself, or any owner/shareholder, employee, etc, who is physically located in the state where the corporation is registered.

> **HOT TIP**: Most states allow you to use a **registered corporate agent**, which is a special type of business that receives lawsuits summons on behalf of companies. They essentially just accept the documents on your behalf, and then pass them along to you. For this simple task, they often charge several hundred dollars per year, and frankly, it's usually a waste of money for a small business. You can simply designate yourself or anyone at your company to do it, for free. And hopefully you aren't the subject of too many lawsuits, so there's not much for a registered agent to do anyway!

Now that that's out of the way, another document you need is called **bylaws**, which set out the rules of operating the corporation. These rules include how and when meetings will be held, and the powers and duties of officers and directors. You generally don't *file* the bylaws anywhere, you just make sure all the shareholders sign it; and you may need to show it to banks or other institutions if they ask for it.

As for the way a corporation is structured, it can be complicated. That said, for small businesses, it's mostly theoretical, essentially just words on paper. Keep this in mind as you read the following. The owners of a corporation are called **shareholders**, who ultimately have all the power. But they delegate much of that power by **electing** the **board of directors**, who make most of the major decisions for the company. The directors in turn appoint **officers**, including

CEO/President, **CFO**, and **Secretary**, to run the day-to-day operations.

For very small businesses, these roles and titles are mostly meaningless. If you are the sole shareholder of the corporation, you would elect yourself as the sole director, and in most states, you can just appoint yourself the CEO/CFO/Secretary. With all these various roles that you are playing, you may find it appropriate to create multiple clones of yourself (we can do that now, right?).

Usually you are required to hold a "meeting" each year (yes, with these various versions of yourselves), and write up a record of that "meeting," which is called the **minutes**. It may sound complicated and quite silly, but again, it's all just on paper.

If you have more than one owner/shareholder, the structure becomes more important, as it will help you resolve disagreements about how to run the company. When you do decide to move in a certain direction, make sure you write that into the minutes, and have everyone sign it. You want to keep everyone on the same page as much as possible, so that people can't later claim that they never authorized this or that. It's also helpful to have a record of when people dissented from certain decisions, as a type of CYA (Cover Your Ass) if things go wrong.

Depending on your state, you may also have to file annual or periodic reports about the corporation. This is sometimes called a **statement of information** or **annual report**. These are usually quite simple, as the government generally just wants to make sure they have up to date information on the address, names of directors, officers, etc of the corporation. The other major obligation for corporations is that most states charge an annual fee or minimum tax regardless of income.

LLC

LLC stands for Limited Liability Company (often people think it stands for "Limited Liability Corporation," which doesn't make any sense, as that would just be a corporation. I have even seen this in high profile newspaper articles, so be careful what you read!) It's relatively simple to set up and operate. Similar to a corporation, to create an LLC, you would file a paper with your state's secretary of state. Only, instead of articles of incorporation, it's called **articles of organization** (sometimes called a certificate of organization or a certificate of formation). At a minimum, it usually must include the LLC's name, address, and an agent for service of process.

Instead of bylaws, you will need an **operating agreement** that states the rules of the road for how the company operates. Similarly to bylaws, you don't file an operating agreement, but make sure all the LLC's owners sign it, and hold on to it to show banks and other institutions if they ask for it at some point.

Owners of an LLC are called **members**. If there is only one owner of the LLC, it is called a **single-member LLC** (as opposed to a **multi-member LLC**). An LLC may also designate **managers** to handle the day-to-day operations, but this is unnecessary in most small LLCs.

You can designate officers such as CEO if you like, but it's not required. Formal minutes are not required either, however, it's still a good idea to keep a record (and have everyone sign) of what is discussed and what is decided regarding the business. As with a corporation, the state may also have annual or periodic informational filing requirements (e.g. a statement of information), and annual fees for LLCs.

And that's about it. It's somewhat simpler than a corporation, with fewer requirements, but you may want to use similar practices as a corporation anyway. Thus, it's not a huge difference in terms of complication and paperwork. It's certainly not as significant a difference as many people make it out to be.

So, what's it gonna be, LLC or corporation?

I won't keep you in suspense any longer: most small businesses would want to do an LLC. (Unless you are a licensed professional in California - see note below). The LLC is simpler, and allows for more options on tax treatment. But if you are planning to be taxed as an S Corp, or, less likely, a C Corp, both which either an LLC or a corporation can do (see Chapter 5), you are probably fine with either.

The costs for an LLC versus a corporation are usually about the same (though in some states the LLC fees are slightly lower, and in other states the *corporation* fees are slightly lower!). As we discussed, there is generally a bit more paperwork for a corporation, but it's not a big deal overall.

Licensed Professionals in California: in California, if you perform certain licensed professional services, including accounting, architecture, medical, etc, you are required to form a **professional corporation** or an LLP rather than an LLC.

Bottom line: Talk to a local lawyer and tax professional, and then you can stop worrying so much about it!

Social enterprise

Are you interested in making a positive impact, or at least avoiding negative impact, with your business? Frankly, the only acceptable answer to this is YES. Otherwise that would mean that you are actively aiming to make the world a worse place, which is, well, not very nice. Anyway, there is an emerging movement to use business as a force for good, or to ensure businesses minimize the harms they may create. These are sometimes called mission-driven businesses, or social enterprises.

A social enterprise is not a radically different business structure, but is more of a modification on the traditional structures. Most social enterprises are structured as one of the following: (1) a traditional corporation or LLC, with B Corp certification; or (2) a special type of corporation such as a Benefit corporation, with or without a B Corp certification.

Before we get into the weeds, I would like to take this opportunity to vent my frustration with the people who coined the terms for social enterprises (including the people at B Lab, and elsewhere). While I am very appreciative of the work they did to bring these concepts to life and law, I have a (friendly) critique for them. As you will see, because they decided to use terms similar to those for existing structures (benefit corporation vs public benefit corporation), as well as similar terms for things which are completely different (benefit corporation vs B corporation), there is much potential for confusion. I will do my best to explain everything, but these people have made this much more difficult than it needs to be!

OK, rant over. I feel better now. But please, can we make some changes?

What is a Certified B Corp?

A **Certified B Corporation** (often abbreviated "**B Corp**") is a business or organization that has been certified by the non-profit organization B Lab as meeting certain requirements as to various aspects related to the environment, the community, and employees. Even though it uses the term "corporation," it is a certification, *not* a legal structure. It is often confused with a **benefit corporation**, which *is* a legal structure. A company can be a Certified B Corp with or without being a benefit corporation. It doesn't even have to be a corporation at all! Sometimes a company can be an LLC or any other type of entity and still be a Certified B Corp.

Some examples of other certifications that a company may pursue in addition to the B Corp are Fair Trade Certified, Food Alliance Certified, USDA Certified Organic, 1% For the Planet, etc.

What is a benefit corporation?

A **benefit corporation** is a particular type of legal structure for a business. It is based on a regular for-profit corporation, with a few modifications. The biggest difference between a benefit corporation and a regular corporation is that the benefit corporation expands the allowable activities. To explain this, we need to briefly discuss the basis of a corporation.

A regular for-profit corporation is legally obligated to maximize value for its shareholders. This means that if the corporation is doing things that may make slightly less profits than it could, the shareholders can sue the corporation to stop this. For example, if a grocery company operating as a corporation wants to focus its efforts on a lower income market to provide that community better access to fresh produce, but where it may make less money than a higher income neighborhood, the shareholders may be within their legal rights to stop this action.

In contrast, a benefit corporation removes this restriction, and allows – actually *requires* – the corporation to pursue both a profit and a positive impact on society and the environment, and to consider the effects of its actions on the community, the environment, employees, consumers, and other stakeholders. The shareholders of a benefit corporation may not sue simply because they are not making as much profit as they could.

The benefit corporation must also produce an annual report, available to the public, describing how well it has met its impact goals. Other than these requirements and expanded scope of decision-making, the benefit corporation is essentially the same as a traditional corporation. The initial and annual costs are usually similar as well.

Like other corporations, the benefit corporation structure is created through the state. As of January 2021, 37 states allow the creation of benefit corporations. In contrast, the B Corp certification is granted by the non-profit B Lab.

Another potential area of confusion is that there is an existing type of structure called a **public benefit corporation**, which is very different from a benefit corporation (seriously, why would they call it that?). A public benefit corporation is a non-profit entity, usually a 501(c)(3), which operates under quite different rules than for-profit entities like benefit corporations. There are major differences in terms of taxes, funding sources, ownership, and even how the entity is allowed to make certain decisions.

Benefit Corporation vs Non-profit Public Benefit Corporation

	Benefit Corporation	Non-profit Public Benefit Corporation
Taxes	Not tax exempt, but may be able to deduct charitable giving as business expense	May apply for tax exemption as 501(c)(3)
Funding	May receive investments in exchange for equity Not eligible for most grant funding; donations NOT tax deductible for donors	No investments in exchange for equity Eligible for grant funding; donations are tax deductible for donors
Restrictions	Fewer restrictions on activities and decision making	Many rules and regulations; limitations on activities; can't make major decisions without approval from independent board members
Ownership	Founders and others can get unlimited financial benefit from the business	All assets and funds are irrevocably dedicated to the mission; founders and staff can only get salaries
Set up and maintenance	Easier and less expensive to set up and maintain	More complicated and expensive set up and maintain

Benefit corporation vs Certified B Corp

A benefit corporation is a legal structure, while a B Corp is a certification which is *in addition to* a legal structure.

Benefit Corporation vs Certified B Corp

	Benefit Corporation	Certified B Corp
What is it?	Legal structure	Certification
How do you get it?	File with your state's Secretary of State	Apply to B Lab
Initial costs	Varies by state ($50-$500)	$1000+ (depending on annual revenue) plus legal structure costs
Annual costs	Varies by state ($0-$800)	$1000+ (depending on annual revenue) plus legal structure costs
Benefits	• Freedom to pursue non-financial goals • Marketing • Discounts	• Membership in B Corp community • Marketing • Discounts

What are the benefits to being certified as a B Corp?

- marketing: many customers prefer to patronize certified B Corps
- discounts: many businesses cater to Certified B Corps and offer them discounts
- government contracts: some local and state governments favor certified B Corps over traditional companies
- funding: many investors specifically look to invest in B Corps

What are the disadvantages to being certified as a B Corp?

- annual fee is $1,000+ depending on the company's revenue
- must also set up legal structure (usually benefit corporation), which adds to costs
- requirements for certification somewhat strict

What are the benefits to being structured as a benefit corporation?

Similar to a Certified B Corp, there are advantages to benefit corporations with regard to:

- marketing
- discounts
- government contracts.

Benefit corporations also have a unique advantage:

- legal freedom to pursue non-financial goals, including environment and community

What are the disadvantages of being structured as a benefit corporation?

- potential legal liability for directors and officers for failing to consider the environment or other constituencies in making certain decisions.

Do B Corps or benefit corporations have tax advantages?

Unlike non-profits, neither Certified B Corps nor benefit corporations are tax exempt. But the IRS has indicated that social enterprises may be able to deduct charitable giving as a *business expense*. This is an advantage over non-social enterprises, which may only deduct charitable giving as a *charitable deduction*, which is limited to 25% of taxable income.

How Do I Properly Set Up and Maintain My Business Structure?

Once again, if you are a sole proprietor and intend to stay that way, there's not really much setup, other than possible requirements to get certain licenses and permits. For a partnership, the setup essentially just involves drawing up a partnership agreement. As for the entities, the specifics vary by state. The following is a look at the general steps to take to set up a sole proprietorship, partnership, LLC, and corporation.

For more specific information, check your state's secretary of state website. To really make sure you do it right, it's best to get help from a business lawyer.

Before we get into the *how*, I want you to understand the *why* – how important it is to set things up *properly*. Then, hopefully, you will have more motivation to pay attention to the section about the actual steps to do it right!

What are the consequences if I don't properly set up and maintain my business structure?

Dire. What, did you expect me to say everything would be fine? Regardless of your business structure, if you fail to take the required and recommended steps, you could face significant fines and other penalties from the IRS and numerous other government agencies. You could be forced to give up more profits than you intended to your collaborators, or you could face lawsuits from customers or clients.

If you do have a legal entity, there's even more at stake. Often – way too often – people register their entity with the state, and then think they are good and covered, and go about their business. But if it's not set up and maintained properly with all the necessary procedures, it's essentially useless. Specifically, the primary benefits of the entity – personal asset protection and tax reduction – could be eliminated if you don't make sure to dot the i's and cross the t's. It's like buying an expensive alarm system for your house, that you don't turn on, while a burglar steals all your valuables.

How could your entity lose these benefits? Let's look at a few scenarios. If you forget to file your annual or periodic informational reports with the secretary of state (e.g. statement of information), the state could declare the entity as suspended or not in good standing.

Or say you ignore formalities like having an **operating agreement** for your LLC, or you **commingle** moneys, using your business account for personal items and vice versa. And then you get sued. Perhaps you say no worries, they can't touch my personal assets. But the court can see right through this, literally. It can **pierce the veil** of the LLC, and declare that you are not treating the entity as separate from your personal assets, and thus the law will not treat it as separate either. All of your personal assets could be up for grabs in the lawsuit!

OK, let's say you've got it all under control, and you're doing everything by the book. But all that effort could still be for naught, if you work with clients under just your own name and you never even mention the LLC. In this situation, the LLC's umbrella is not extending to you for this work, which could leave you, well, soaked.

Have I sufficiently alarmed you about the consequences of failing to meet the legal requirements of your business structure? Good. Now let's talk about the how of it all.

Slicing up the pie (and other arrangements with co-owners)

If you have co-founders, you will need to establish how much of the business each person will own, what everyone's roles and responsibilities will be, and how you will make decisions regarding operating the business. Depending on which form your business takes, these characteristics will be reflected in different documents.

In a partnership, all of the above should be written down in a partnership agreement. At a minimum, the partnership agreement should include: purpose of the partnership (what kind of business activities it will carry out); when the partners can take profits (**draws**); management duties and powers; what happens when a partner wants to exit, or the others want to remove a partner; how disputes among the partners will be resolved; contributions of each partner (money, work, equipment, etc.); and percentage of the business each partner will own (share of profits or losses).

In an LLC, most of this would be included in the operating agreement. The ownership and contributions are usually recorded in what is called the **capital contributions table** ("cap table"). This simply lists the percentage ownership of each owner, and the various contributions each owner will make to the business (not just capital - money, equipment, etc - but services as well).

And in a corporation, you would include most of these provisions in the bylaws. Ownership and contributions are reflected in **share certificates**, which designate how many shares each shareholder owns, and the **stock ledger**, which is simply a record of the shares each person received, and the contributions they made or will make in exchange.

My clients often get more than a bit excited when they get the ornately decorated and official-looking share certificates with their name and the thousands of shares of the company they own. The actual number of shares a company issues is arbitrary, as long as it distributes the ownership proportionally. If it makes you happy, you can issue yourself a million shares! Or keep things more down to earth with, say, 1,000 shares. You do you.

What are the actual steps of setting up and maintaining my business structure?

The specifics of forming a sole proprietorship, partnership, LLC, or corporation, and keeping it in compliance varies by state. Here are the general steps to properly set up and maintain these structures:

Sole proprietorship

Setting up

1. Make sure this structure is best for your situation – talk to a business lawyer about the legal structure and a CPA/tax professional about the tax treatment.
2. Obtain EIN (see Chap 6).
3. File for required licenses, permits, or DBA (see Chap 6).

4. Open a business bank account.

Ongoing

1. Keep finances separate from your personal finances.
2. File and pay taxes and fees (see Chap 5).
3. If necessary, renew any licenses, permits, or DBA.

General partnership

Setting up

1. Make sure this structure is best for your situation – talk to a business lawyer about the legal structure and a CPA/tax professional about the tax treatment.
2. Properly draft and execute a partnership agreement.
3. Obtain EIN (see Chap 6).
4. File for required licenses, permits, or DBA (see Chap 6).
5. Open a bank account in the name of the partnership.

Ongoing

1. Keep finances separate from personal finances.
2. Make sure contracts are in the name of the partnership.
3. File and pay taxes and fees (see Chap 5).
4. If necessary, renew any licenses, permits, or DBA.

LLC

Setting up

1. Make sure this structure is best for your situation – talk to a business lawyer about the legal structure and a CPA/tax professional about the tax treatment.

2. Properly file founding document (usually called articles of organization) with your state's Secretary of State.
3. Obtain EIN (see Chap 6).
4. If applicable, file with IRS to select tax treatment. For tax treatments of sole proprietorship or partnership, no filing necessary. For S corp tax treatment, file Form 2553. For C corp tax treatment, file Form 8832.
5. Prepare and sign operating agreement.
6. Prepare other initial documents, including resolutions, member certificates, etc.
7. File for any required licenses or permits (see Chap 6).
8. Open a bank account in the full name of the LLC.

Ongoing

1. Keep finances separate from your personal finances.
2. Make sure contracts are in the full name of the LLC.
3. Use full LLC name on your website, business cards, etc.
4. Properly file and pay taxes and fees (see Chap 5).
5. Properly file any forms (such as statements of information) that are required annually or every so often.
6. If necessary, renew any licenses, permits, or DBA.

Corporation

Setting up

1. Make sure this structure is best for your situation – talk to a business lawyer about the legal structure and a CPA/tax professional about the tax treatment.

2. Properly file founding document (articles of incorporation) with your state's Secretary of State.
3. If applicable, file paperwork with IRS to select your tax treatment. The corporation is automatically a C corporation unless it elects to be an S corporation. For S corporation tax treatment, file Form 2553.
4. Prepare and sign bylaws.
5. Prepare other initial documents, including resolutions, stock certificates, etc.
6. Obtain EIN (see Chap 6).
7. Properly file for any required licenses or permits (see Chap 6).
8. Open a bank account in the name of the corporation.

Ongoing

1. Keep finances separate from your personal finances.
2. Make sure contracts are in the name of the corporation.
3. Use the official corporation name on your website, business cards, etc.
4. Properly file and pay taxes and fees (see Chap 5).
5. Properly file any forms (such as statements of information) that are required annually or every so often.
6. If necessary, renew any licenses, permits, or DBA.

Can I save money on taxes and fees by forming my entity in a different state?

Many people think they have a brilliant idea to save some money by forming their entity in a state with the lowest costs.

The short answer is that won't work. If you register your entity in another state, your home state will probably find out and require you to also register and pay the fees and taxes in your state. This means you would be paying the fees and taxes for BOTH states!

Let's say you live in California and you want to avoid its highest-in-the-country $800 annual minimum tax. So you register an LLC in Arizona. Sooner or later, you will get some notices in the mail from the state of California saying that you must register your Arizona LLC in California and pay that $800.

"The hardest thing in the world to understand is income taxes."

— Albert Einstein

5 - Business Taxes Are... Taxing

I'm not going to sugarcoat it: business taxes can be a challenge. Yes, you can (and probably should) hire a tax professional to handle your business taxes. But there are many tax tasks (just trying to say that is a challenge!) that you simply cannot delegate. Your tax person is not going to accompany you on every business related shopping trip to make sure you save your receipts, or ride along on every business related car trip to make sure you log your mileage. That would be a *very* dedicated and probably *very* expensive tax pro. The good news is that there are apps and other technologies to help manage these ongoing tasks. For example, you can use QuickBooks or FreshBooks for accounting and expense tracking, and MileIQ to automatically track your mileage.

If you neglect your tax responsibilities, it can have serious legal consequences. Not only could the IRS and other tax agencies come after you, but, as we discussed, you could lose any personal asset protection you had with your entity. Meaning, if clients successfully sue your business, they could have a claim to your personal assets.

Now that I have sufficiently scared you, the reality is that only about 2-3% of small businesses are **audited**, or investigated, by the IRS.[2] But are you willing to roll the dice? Aside from the risks, all this extra effort could pay off, as small businesses can potentially get some nice tax advantages.

How Do Taxes Work for Small Business?

Most employees have one income source, they fill out a W-4 form once, and receive a W-2 form each year clearly showing how much they got paid and how much taxes were taken out. Easy peasy, right?

For the self-employed, not so easy. In order to properly file your taxes, and actually to properly run your business, you must track and categorize all business income and expenses. The IRS wants to know how you are making your money and how you are spending it. They want to know specifics including how much you are spending on the direct costs of your goods (if you sell products), how much you are spending on office supplies, advertising, employee or contractor compensation, and more.

You can outsource most of this to a good bookkeeper or accountant, but you will need to explain to them what's what. They will not necessarily know how to categorize an expense at Target, even if you send them a copy of the receipt (sometimes the item descriptions on receipts aren't helpful – on one of my recent Target receipts, it just said "Picadilly." What is that?). So, as a business owner, you need to have a good understanding of all of this, and oversee the finances even when you delegate these tasks.

Gross income and not so gross (net) income

Gross income may sound like a dirty dollar bill, but it really just refers to all the money you have received from clients and customers, before accounting for business expenses. **Net income**, or **profits**, is the amount you have left after your business expenses. Generally you are taxed only on your net income, although certain taxes may be applied based on your gross income. In the next section, we will discuss how taxes are generally calculated based on net income.

Does business income get reported to the IRS?

The IRS is not an omnipresent, omniscient Big Brother, but they do know things. Much of their information comes from the aptly-named **informational returns**. For example, employers are required to tell the IRS how much they paid each employee every year, which they do on an informational return you may be familiar with – the **W-2 form** (employees also receive a copy).

So, the IRS already knows how much an employee made in the year, and can tax them accordingly. This is why there's an ongoing debate about whether the IRS should simply do the tax filings on behalf of these taxpayers, rather than put this responsibility on them. There's good arguments on both sides, as the IRS does not know about many life circumstances that can affect the calculation of taxes, such as getting married or divorced, having children, etc. But I digress.

In contrast to employment income, income for businesses and self-employed people is primarily based on self-report. This means you, the business owner, must keep track of all business income – including payments to you by credit card, checks, cash, crypto, etc. – and report it on your annual tax filing. That said, certain informational returns do pick up some of this activity, and as of January 2022, the IRS is collecting even more of this information from third parties.

If you take payments through a payment processor, e-commerce platform, or third party settlement organization, such as PayPal, Venmo, Square, Stripe, Zelle, Etsy, Shopify, etc., these services must now send the IRS (and you) an information return if you have received over $600 on the platform during the tax year. Using the **1099 form**, they report the total amount you received on the platform during the year.

In certain circumstances, your clients also may need to file a 1099 to report their payments to you if the total they paid you is over $600 for the year. This would apply if your business provides services (as opposed to products) to clients, and you are not taxed as either an S corporation or C corporation. If this applies, your clients may ask you to fill out a W-9 form which collects information that allows them to fill out the 1099 form.

Sometimes the client won't file the 1099 even though they are supposed to, possibly because they don't know about this requirement. Either way, it's not your responsibility, so don't worry about this. The bottom line, so to speak, is that you are required to self-report all income regardless of whether it is reported to the IRS by third parties.

Deducing business deductions

Now for a happier topic. Probably the biggest tax advantage for business owners is the business expense deduction. You can deduct ("write off") business expenses to reduce your taxable income. For example, if you earn $100,000 gross, but you spent $20,000 on things like supplies and equipment, getting around, etc., your business income is really $80,000. So, you are taxed on that $80K, not $100K. If your **effective tax rate** (income tax + self-employment, etc) is, say, 30%, your tax bill would be around 24K (30% of 80K) rather than 30K, saving you about 6 grand. Not too bad.

If you have significant business costs in a particular year, you may be able to avoid taxes altogether for that year. A new business which has significant startup costs may have little to no profit, even if it brought in good revenue. Let's say you did $50K in sales, but to get that, you had to spend big on marketing, equipment, etc., which added up to around $50K. What are your taxes now? ZERO. Because you had no profit, there's nothing to tax!

Does this mean you should spend as much as you can on your business in order to reduce your tax bill? Certainly not. Your total take-home amount after taxes is generally still greater without any business expenses.

As an example, say you have revenue of $150K, and an effective tax rate of 30%. You are considering spending 50K on upgraded equipment, but you may be able to make it work with what you already have. If you buy the equipment, your net income is 100K, so your taxes are 30K. Including the cost of the equipment, the amount left in your bank account is 70K (150 minus 50 minus 30). If, on the other hand, you decide not to buy the equipment, you would pay 45K in taxes (30% of 150), leaving you with 105K (35K more than 70K) in your account.

Another issue is that business expenses must be considered legitimate to the IRS. What exactly does this include? It all depends on your business, but generally it includes things like marketing, equipment, business related rent, etc. Basically, if you can make a solid argument that an expense is necessary and directly related to your business, then you can probably deduct it. Talk to a tax professional for more.

Do I need an LLC or corporation to be able to take business expenses?

No! This is a very common misconception. As long as you are operating a legitimate business, whether as a sole proprietor, partnership, LLC, corporation, etc., you can deduct your business expenses.

Paying (and paying and paying) your taxes

Even if you do get 1099s, your taxes are not automatically calculated or set aside by the payer. You, the small business, are blessed and cursed with this responsibility. Finance people say you should set aside about 25-30% of your expected profits, as this is a rough estimate of how much you will pay in taxes.

Perhaps you can put it in a cookie jar labeled TAXES, next to a cookie jar filled with actual cookies that you can eat to

Quarterly Estimated Tax Payments

Period	Due date*
January 1 - March 31	April 15
April 1 - May 31	June 15
June 1 - August 31	September 15
September 1 - December 31	January 15 (following year)

*Note: If any due date falls on a Saturday, Sunday, or legal holiday, the due date is on the next day that's not a Saturday, Sunday, or legal holiday.

make yourself feel better about paying all those taxes. That money (and probably the cookies) won't be sitting in the jar too long. This comes as a shock to many new small business owners, but unlike employees, you don't pay taxes just once per year. For federal (and some state) taxes, you must make payments each quarter (January, April, June, September) based on the estimated taxes you owe from the prior quarter.

To determine the amount for your **quarterly estimated tax payments**, first you need to estimate and project how much you will earn in profits this year. Then estimate the taxes you will owe on this year's income; you may want to use the tax rate you paid last year as a rough guide. Divide the total estimated taxes by four. That is the amount you would likely pay this year in April, June, September, and next year in January. When you actually do your taxes by April of next year, if you overpaid on your estimated payments, you will get a refund. If you underpaid, you will owe the difference, and possibly a penalty.

Before you start complaining about this extra requirement (although who doesn't enjoy complaining sometimes), compare this to employees, who in effect pay estimated taxes 12-24 times per year (or whenever they get paid). Sure, it's all done automatically for them, but still, at least you get to hold on to that money for a bit longer. And if you think about it, it's really just three extra dates to keep track of, since the April due date is the same as for everyone's individual (personal) taxes.

Another big shock for new entrepreneurs is that small business owners must pay **self-employment tax**, which is an extra 7.65% that employees don't pay. What is this madness? Well, employees have **payroll taxes** taken out each paycheck. In addition to estimated income tax withheld, this also includes taxes which pay for Social Security and Medicare. While this tax is 15.3%, employers must pay half of this for employees, so employees only pay 7.65%.[3] Yet, as you are both employer (of yourself) and employee (that's right, more clones of yourself!), you must pay the full 15ish percent. Oh, the price of freedom.

What Tax Treatment Should I Use?

So far, we have been discussing how taxes work for small business in general. Now, let's talk about specific tax treatments and what each would mean for you. The tax status you choose can have a significant effect on your bottom line. You should also consider the amount of paperwork and time required for the various tax treatments. Here's what you can expect with each of these.

What are all the tax treatments?

Remember that tax treatment is not the same as legal structure. Once a legal structure is created, you can then choose a tax treatment to apply. There are essentially four types of tax treatments that small businesses should be familiar with: sole proprietorship, partnership, C corporation (sometimes referred to as simply being taxed as a "corporation"), and the good ol' S corporation. While the most relevant will be the sole proprietorship, partnership, and the S Corp, it's important to at least be familiar with the C Corp, as it will help you understand how the others work.

Taxed as… a sole proprietorship

Being taxed as a sole proprietorship is very simple. There is no tax at the entity level (since there is no entity). You, the business owner, are taxed on the profits from your business (income minus expenses) through your personal income taxes.

Taxed as… a partnership

Partnerships are taxed by **pass-through taxation**. Pass-through tax treatment simply means the business profit is not taxed at the entity level; instead, it passes through the business, on to the business *owners*. The business owners are taxed based on their individual share of the profits, which is usually based on percentage ownership of the business.

As an example, say Maria and Jo are partners in MarJo, and Maria owns 60% of the business, while Jo owns 40%. If MarJo brings in profits of 100K, MarJo does not pay taxes on this. Instead, Maria would pay taxes on her 60K of income, and Jo would pay taxes on her 40K income.

Taxed as... a C Corporation

Very few small businesses will want to use C corporation taxation. Here's why. As a C corp, the corporation itself is taxed on its profits. When you move the income of the corporation to yourself as an owner of the corporation (called **taking an owner's draw** or paying the owners **dividends**), this same income is taxed again on your personal income taxes! This situation is known, appropriately, as **double taxation**, and you will almost certainly want to avoid it by choosing another tax treatment.

That said, there is a way around the double taxation of a C corp. If you pay all the corporate earnings out to yourself and the other owners as salary, then there would be no corporate profit (since salary is a business expense), and thus no tax at the corporate level. You would just be subject to personal income taxes on that salary as if you were an employee. While this arrangement may be beneficial in certain circumstances, it's much simpler and usually more cost-effective to be taxed as an S corporation.

Taxed as... an S Corporation

The S Corp is a special kind of magic. Like a partnership, an S Corp has pass-through taxation. So, it avoids the double taxation of a C corporation. But it gets better. In a partnership, the owner's draws are considered self-employment income, which, as you know, is subject to self-employment tax. In contrast, as a corporation, when you take an owner's draw, it is not considered self-employment income, it's considered **dividends**, just like when you own stock in the stock market. Since you don't pay self-employment tax on dividends, you save over 15% on this money, which can add up to thousands of dollars!

While you would naturally want to pay out everything as dividends, it doesn't quite work that way. The IRS requires you to pay yourself a "reasonable" salary before paying dividends. The definition of reasonable salary is one of those gray areas, but it's generally based on an average salary for your specific profession or industry.

Here's an example of how it can work. Let's say you earn $80,000 net income from your business. Without an S Corp, you could end up paying around 35% tax on that (assuming 20% income tax + 15% self-employment tax), or $28,000. Now, with an S Corp: Perhaps a reasonable salary is $50,000, so the other $30,000 would be dividends. The $50K may be taxed at around 35% ($17.5K); while the $30K would just be taxed at the income tax rate, with NO self-employment tax, ($30K x .2 = $6K); for a total of $23.5K. You just saved $4,500 ($28K-$23.5K)! Go buy yourself something nice. Actually, you should invest that back into the business.

LLC (NOT a tax treatment)

Note that LLC is NOT a type of tax treatment. An LLC must *choose* to be taxed as follows: an LLC with a single owner can be treated as a sole proprietorship[T], S corporation, or C corporation; and if there are multiple owners, it can be treated as a partnership[T], S corporation, or C corporation.

If it chooses nothing, then by default, the LLC is treated as a sole proprietorship[T] (if one owner), or a partnership[T] (if more than one owner). It drives me a bit nuts, but even some lawyers and CPAs talk about a business being "taxed as an LLC." This is not the proper way to describe it, and it just confuses people. When you read and hear this, keep in mind that it generally means the LLC's default tax treatment as either sole proprietorship[T] or partnership[T].

An LLC taxed as a sole proprietorship is usually considered a **disregarded entity**. This may sound problematic, or like you are being tossed aside like some garbage, but that's not necessarily the case at all. It simply means that the IRS disregards or ignores the LLC and applies the same tax treatment as if you were a sole proprietorship. However, states generally do not disregard the LLC, and many states impose a minimum tax or fee on the LLC each year.

When an LLC is taxed as an S corp or C corp, the entity is often simply referred to as an S corp or C corp. This is more misleading terminology! A more accurate (yet admittedly cumbersome) way to describe it is an "LLC taxed as an S corp" or an "LLC taxed as a C corp."

Which tax treatment will help save the most money on taxes?

Now that we have the basics covered, which tax treatment should you choose to get the most bang for your buck?

> **HOT TIP:** If you are just starting out and/or you aren't making much profit yet, you would probably want to be taxed as a sole proprietorship (if it's just you) or partnership (if you have co-owners).

What if you're starting to bring in some real dough? (Really, it's time for a bagel or croissant or something.) Depending on what a reasonable salary is for your profession or industry, this is the threshold at which it may make sense to become an S corp. This is generally a minimum of $50K (after expenses), but it may be as high as $100K. Basically, if you are doing better financially than your peers, congratulations. You may have reached "Level S" (I just made that up). But seriously, talk to a tax pro to see if you could save some serious cash.

Papers and deadlines

Another concern in choosing a tax treatment is the amount of paperwork required, which can certainly be... taxing (I won't do that pun again, I promise). Sole proprietorships generally have the least paperwork, usually just a **Schedule C** worksheet added to the **1040 form** that all taxpayers must fill out. Partners in a partnership add the **Schedule E** to their 1040, but the partnership itself has an additional requirement to report the overall partnership earnings separately (**1065** form).

S corps require quite a bit of extra tax work: the owners include Schedule E on the 1040, and the S corp itself must file the **1120S** form, which can be complicated. As for a C corp, you would use the **1120** form, a very complicated document.

While you could (and probably should) pay someone to do your business taxes, your tax preparer will need you to supply detailed business records. The more complex the form, the more information they will need from you. And the more the tax preparer will charge you!

In addition to paperwork, there's a slight difference in the actual filing dates of said papers. If you are taxed as a sole proprietor or C Corporation, the due date for your business taxes is April 15. This conveniently coincides with both the due date for your personal taxes, and the first estimated tax payment. But if you are taxed as a partnership or an S Corp, your business taxes are due March 15 instead. Then you would have 5 essential dates to keep track of.

The following pages include calendars for when filings are due, and the paperwork required, depending on your tax treatment.

Tax Calendar for multi-member LLC/partnership/S corp

Due Date*	Description
January 15	Pay estimated tax for Sept through Dec of prior year
March 15	File business taxes for prior year's income (pay any remaining taxes or receive refund on top of estimated payments made)
April 15	Pay estimated tax for Jan through March File personal taxes & business taxes for prior year's income (and pay any remaining taxes or receive refund for overpayment)
June 15	Pay estimated tax for April and May
September 15	Pay estimated tax for June through August

*Note: If any due date falls on a Saturday, Sunday, or legal holiday, the due date is on the next day that's not a Saturday, Sunday, or legal holiday.

Tax Calendar for Sole Proprietor/ C Corporation

Due Date*	Description
January 15	Pay estimated tax for Sept through Dec of prior year
April 15	Pay estimated tax for Jan through March File personal taxes & business taxes for prior year's income (and pay any remaining taxes or receive refund of overpayments)
June 15	Pay estimated tax for April and May
September 15	Pay estimated tax for June through August

*Note: If any due date falls on a Saturday, Sunday, or legal holiday, the due date is on the next day that's not a Saturday, Sunday, or legal holiday.

Paperwork for Various Tax Treatments

Tax treatment	Fill out for clients	Receive from clients	Business entity files w/ IRS	Each business owner files w/ IRS
Sole proprietorship	W-9	1099	N/A	Quarterly est taxes + 1040 + Sched C
General partnership	W-9	1099	1065 + K-1s	Quarterly est taxes + 1040 + Sched E
S corp	N/A	N/A	1120S + K-1s	Quarterly est taxes + 1040 + Sched E
C corp	N/A	N/A	Quarterly est taxes + 1120	Quarterly est taxes + 1040 + Sched D

What if I miss a deadline?

If you don't pay the right amount of estimated tax by each due date, you may be charged a penalty, even if you're due a refund when you file your income tax return. As for filing the actual tax return, you are entitled to a 6-month automatic extension. But if you think you owe taxes at the time the return is due, you should estimate what you owe and pay it. Otherwise, if you pay it 6 months later, you will be charged a penalty and interest.

OK so after I do all that, I'm done with taxes, right?

Wellllll.... maybe not. We have now covered the basics of federal tax for business. Depending on your state and city, you may have additional tax requirements. For the most part, these are nowhere near as burdensome as the federal situation.

State tax

As we have discussed, the majority of states impose an annual "minimum tax" or fee on LLCs and corporations. Most states also impose income tax on business *owners* for their business earnings.

Local tax

Your city or county may tax the business as well. But these tax rates are also generally much lower than federal rates, and many localities exempt small business from these taxes.

Sales tax

If you sell any goods (even digital things like eBooks), you may be required to collect sales tax from your customers and send this to the government. You are really just passing along this money from the customer to the government, and it doesn't come out of your profits. So it's not a tax for you, but simply an administrative requirement as part of the "seller's permit" requirements (see Chapter 6).

Is All This Worth It?

Now that we have covered all that, most businesses will not have any other tax requirements. You can exhale now. In fact, take a moment to do some breathing exercises, or get up and stretch. We're making lots of progress here, and you deserve a break!

Still, at this point you may be wishing for the simpler ways of the W-2 employee who doesn't need to deal with all this. But, consider the benefits. Compared to an employee who has their taxes automatically sent to the IRS each paycheck, you get up to 4.5 months of extra time to keep this money. With the right fiscal discipline, you can use it as an interest-free loan, or maybe even do some short-term investing. When taking into account business expense deductions, an

S Corp, etc, you may come out on top. Again, it all depends on your specific situation.

So How Do I Actually File My Taxes?

As for specifics about *how* to prepare your taxes, how much you owe, how you could reduce your tax liability, etc., these are all good questions – for a tax professional such as a CPA (certified public accountant) or possibly a bookkeeper who is well versed in taxes.

I often get questions about taxes, and I generally defer to the tax people. Most lawyers are not numbers people (that's why we went to law school). While tax lawyers are an exception, they mostly handle **controversies** and **audits**, where the government says you didn't pay enough taxes, or **resolutions**, where you need to work out a payment plan or settlement for your taxes. For tax prep and related questions, stick with the numbers people.

Taxes Recap

The main takeaways here are to keep good records of all business income and expenses, and properly file and pay your federal, state, and local taxes each quarter/year, as applicable. Taking care of all this will ensure that you don't pay more in taxes than you need to, and will help keep the tax authorities off your back.

Now that you know the basics of business entities and business taxes, it's time to "choose your own adventure."

You may want to go back to the diagrams in Chapter 4 that show the process of creating a legal structure and tax treatment. What are you thinking in terms of an entity and tax treatment? _____. You can also write this in the worksheet at the end of the book. Be sure to discuss your preferences with a lawyer and tax professional.

"Character cannot be developed in ease and quiet. Only through experience of trial and suffering can the soul be strengthened, ambition inspired and success achieved."

- Helen Keller

6 – Let Me See Your License and Registration

No, you're not being pulled over by highway patrol. As a small business, you may have certain licensing and registration requirements, depending on your activities and the city and state in which you do business.

Do I Need to Register My Business?

"Registering" a business can mean several different things, and there may be various government agencies to "register" with, depending on your circumstances. This includes incorporating, or registering as an entity with the state, which we have discussed above. It also may include getting a local business license (aka business tax registration); DBA; seller's permit; EIN (Employer Identification Number); getting a license or permit for your professional or business activities; registering as an employer; or getting a zoning permit. Following is more details on each of these.

Local Business License and Tax Filings

Many cities and counties require businesses to pay local business tax. This may be administered through either an annual tax filing, or a requirement to get a **business license** that you must renew each year or so. It is sometimes known by other names, including business operating license, or business tax registration certificate. Check with your city and/or county for more.

The ABCs of the DBA

A common misconception is that the DBA is the same as the business license. It is not. Depending on your situation, you may need to file a DBA statement in addition to getting a business license.

In some states the DBA is known as a **trade name** (not to be confused with trademark), fictitious business name, fictitious name, assumed business name, or assumed name. The specifics vary by state, but the way it generally works is that if you are a sole proprietor and you are using a business name that does not include your personal legal name, you need to file a DBA statement (aka fictitious business name statement, or trade name statement, etc). If you are a partnership and you are using a business name that does not include the names of all the partners, you need to file a DBA statement.

Here are some examples of when you may or may not need to file a DBA statement:

1. You are Frida Kahlo, and your sole proprietorship is Frida Kahlo Arts. You almost certainly do not need to file a DBA statement.
2. You are Bruce Wayne and your sole proprietorship is Wayne Enterprises. You *may* need to file a DBA statement.

3. You are Jerry Seinfeld and you have a general partnership with George Costanza called Vandelay Industries. You will need to file a DBA statement.
4. You are Maria Dunder and you have a general partnership with Julia Mifflin, called Dunder Mifflin. You *may* need to file a DBA statement.
5. You are Maria Dunder and you have a general partnership with Julia Mifflin, called Maria Dunder & Julia Mifflin Paperworks. You probably do not need to file a DBA statement.

A common misconception is that if you have an LLC or corporation, you need to file a DBA in addition to the LLC/corporate paperwork. This is usually not the case. You would only need to file it if you want to use a name *other than* the official name of the LLC or corporation. If your business is Monkeying Around Productions LLC, and you are holding yourself out to the public as Monkeying Around Productions LLC, you do NOT need to file a DBA.

On the other hand, say you wanted to start a 2nd production company, related to birds, called Tweeter Productions. You could set up a second entity as Tweeter Productions LLC. Or, instead of spending the extra money and time on that, you could simply file a DBA statement for Tweeter Productions under the existing entity, Monkeying Around Productions LLC.

The DBA filing would list Monkeying Around Productions LLC as the owner of Tweeter Productions. You would be operating both businesses through this LLC, although it would appear to the public as two separate entities. This may sound like a great 2-for-1 deal, an easy way to maintain two businesses for the price of one. But it may not be best for your situation. If, for example, you will have different funding sources or investors for each company, you may need to have a separate LLC for each.

Now, how do you actually file the DBA statement? In some states the DBA is filed with the state's secretary of state; in other states it is filed with the **county clerk** in the count(ies) in which you operate.

Registering Your Professional or Business Activities

In order to offer certain services or goods, or to use certain titles (like therapist, engineer, architect, etc.), you may need to get a special **professional license** (sometimes called an **occupational license**), permit, registration, or certification. Or, if you serve or sell food, you likely need to get a permit/license from the local health department. Sometimes there are optional certifications you can obtain, which are not legally required, but may help to boost your reputation.

If you have already been providing certain professional services as an employee, you may already have this covered. Perhaps you have been working as a licensed architect for a firm for several years, but now you are ready to BYOB (be your own boss) and start your own firm. In this case, you would probably not need to take further steps with regard to architecture licensure. But do check with your state's licensing board, as they sometimes require you to notify them that you are starting a firm.

If your services are at all related to a licensed field, and you do not have the proper licensure, you can either obtain it, or avoid doing any licensed activities. Performing certain services without complying with the requirements could subject you to significant fines and/or even prison time. For example, in California, practicing medicine without a license can lead to up to 3 years in state prison!

Let's say you are a nutrition and health consultant, helping people make smart choices in terms of food and supplements. If you recommend supplements in place of prescription medication, this could be considered to be practicing medicine. Best practices are to clearly state that you are not licensed and you do not perform any licensed activities, and the clients should discuss with a medical doctor before making these decisions. Include this disclaimer in all marketing materials and contracts.

Regulation of Products

If your business sells products, particularly things like food items, health or medical related items, electronics, or items with potentially hazardous chemicals or materials, you may need to get certifications or approvals from the relevant government agency. Food and health products may need approval or inspection by the Food and Drug Administration (FDA) or US Department of Agriculture (USDA), or at the very least the products must comply with labeling regulations. Electronic products may need to obtain approval or certification from the Federal Communications Commission (FCC) to ensure that they do not emit electromagnetic radiation exceeding a certain limit.

To determine what product-specific regulations you must comply with, consult with a lawyer, or the U.S. Small Business Administration (SBA).

Seller's Permit

If you are selling or renting out any tangible goods, you will generally need to get a seller's permit from your state government. This may also be called a sales tax permit or sales tax license. A related requirement is if you purchase goods and resell them, you may need a reseller's permit, or to fill out a resale certificate for each transaction.

As part of the requirement of the seller's permit, you will likely need to collect sales tax from your customers, and then pass this money along to the government (called **remitting**). Many major payment processing platforms and apps such as Etsy, Shopify, etc. have the tax collection built in, automatically calculating the tax based on the customer's zip code. So you don't need to worry about sales tax for items ordered through these platforms.

Registering as an Employer

If you have employees, your state may require that you register as an employer. This state agency may be called the department of labor, or employment development department, or something similar.

Tax ID/EIN

The federal Employer Identification Number (EIN, or sometimes FEIN), is a bit of a misnomer, as it is not only for employers. It is the Tax ID number of the business. Partnerships, LLCs and corporations must have an EIN from the IRS, regardless of whether there are any employees. Although not required for sole proprietors, they have the option to get an EIN. This is a good idea because otherwise you would have to use your personal social security number for business matters. Using your social security number could leave you more vulnerable to identity theft.

> **HOT TIP:** You can get an EIN quickly and at no cost at *IRS.gov*. It just takes about 5-10 minutes. Or a lawyer or tax professional can do this for you, often at low cost or as part of a package of services.

Brick and Mortar Permits

If you perform certain business activities at a physical location, you may need to get a **zoning** or **land use** permit. Check with your city and/or county on this.

Home-based Business

If your business is based out of your home, you may need to get a special permit for this, or at a minimum, comply with the zoning and land use laws. Local zoning and land use laws are quite strict in many localities. They may prohibit any customers or employees from visiting your home, restrict signage on the building, limit the amount of inventory you may hold on the premises, or even restrict certain activities altogether. In addition, if you rent your home or apartment, you may need to get permission from the landlord to conduct business operations there.

If you can't get past these restrictions, you may need to get a space outside your home to run your business. Or if your operations are minimal, you could try fly under the radar while you build your business at home. I'm not advising you to do this, of course. But I'm not *not* advising you to do it.

Can I use a mailbox service or virtual address for my business?

Many home-based businesses use a mailbox service (such as a UPS Store or virtual mailbox) or other mailing address in order to avoid disclosing where the business owner lives. This can work for many business purposes, including the public address for clients and customers. However, banks and some government agencies require a physical address where the business actually operates or where the business owner(s) live. Others may allow the use of a private mailbox service, with an actual street address, but not a P.O. Box with the U.S. Postal Service. When obtaining licenses and permits for your business, be sure to check with each agency on what their rules are on the business address.

"Be yourself. Everyone else is already taken."

— Oscar Wilde

7 – Naming Names: Business Naming and Branding

Small businesses, even if there is just one owner, have an opportunity to build a brand that is larger than themselves (even if it's just themselves). The naming and branding of a business involves DBAs, state registration of business names, and trademark.

DBA

To reiterate the general rules on DBAs, if you are a sole proprietor or partnership and are using a business name that does not include the names of the business owner(s), you generally would need to file a DBA statement. If you have an LLC or corporation, you would only need one if you want to use a name other than the name of the LLC or corporation.

Keep in mind that even if the state or county approves the DBA, this does not give you the full trademark rights to use the name and to prevent others from using it. Trademark is a separate issue, and is handled by a different government agency, the U.S. Patent and Trademark Office. So, what could happen is you may be happily using your Tweeter Productions DBA for awhile, and then along comes Polly who says she registered Tweeter Productions 5 years ago with the Patent and Trademark Office, and claims you must "cease and desist" from using the name. If this turns out to be true, you will likely need to change your name and forfeit your DBA!

State Registration of Business

As you know by now, if you want to form an entity, you must register it with your state's secretary of state. Each state has its own process for registering business entities within the state, including rules for the name of the business. Of course, every state prohibits registering the exact same name as an existing business. There's an obvious conflict there. In most states, you can't use a name that is confusingly similar either. Be sure to read up on all these rules before deciding on a name.

Keep in mind, as with the DBA, a successful registration of a name does not necessarily give you the full rights to use that name. You do not automatically get trademark rights this way. Following is an explanation of how to properly secure these trademark rights.

> **HOT TIP:** Before registering any business with the state, or getting a DBA, you should first ensure you can get the trademark rights. That new business name that you are excited about may already be claimed as a trademark by someone else. If so, you could be forced to change your name and branding that you spent so much time and money on!

Trademark & Other Intellectual Property

Before discussing trademark, a type of intellectual property (IP), it's important to get an overview of intellectual property in general, and distinguish trademark from the other categories of IP. Intellectual property is like other types of property: if you own it, you get to decide what to do with it and to prevent others from using it.

Various intangible things can be considered intellectual property, including creative work such as a drawing or design; a business name or logo; or a concept for a new machine. Each of these fall within separate categories of intellectual property, which work somewhat differently. So, it's essential to understand the differences between the 3 main types of intellectual property: copyright, trademark, and patent.

Trademark law protects your branding, including business name, logos, tag lines, slogans, unique packaging, and anything else that identifies that goods and services are coming from you.

Copyright law protects any original work in a variety of forms, including writings, drawings, photos, music, video, software code, etc. This work can be digital or on paper.

Patent law protects inventions, designs or new methods of doing something. This includes various products and services as hand sanitizer, speed dating, and software.

You may have noticed that some work product can be protected by more than one type of intellectual property. Software may be protected through either/both copyright and/or patent. A business logo is also a design, and as such can be protected by trademark and/or copyright. We will cover copyright and patents in the next chapter.

How does trademark work?

There are two sides of the coin on trademark issues. First, you must make sure not to infringe on others' rights. Second, you should make sure others don't infringe on *your* rights. Thus it is a two-step process.

STEP 1: Make sure your proposed business name, tagline, or logo does not infringe on *others'* trademark rights.

You can't use the same or even similar name that a business is already using for similar goods and services. If you are opening a coffee shop, you might think it would be pretty clever to use the name "Starbuck Coffee," since it is technically different from Starbucks Coffee. But it's **confusingly similar** to the customer, and thus would be trademark infringement.

If you want to use the same or similar name as an existing one, but in a different industry, this is probably fine (but you may have a problem with very famous brands, or brands that are in multiple industries). So, if there is a Sunflower Enterprises that produces widgets, but nobody is using the name Sunflower for consulting services, you likely can use the name Sunflower Consulting. But, you probably can't call yourself Starbucks Consulting.

That reminds me of a funny story. A few years ago I was walking down the street near where I live in Los Angeles, and saw a new coffee shop that called itself "Dumb Starbucks." I went in to check it out, and they had essentially re-created the full Starbucks experience, complete with the mermaid logo and green aprons, except that they put the words "Dumb Starbucks" on everything. It turned out to be a stunt for a TV show, so, not a real coffee shop. Because it was a **parody**, it was not considered trademark infringement, so they could get away with their stunt unscathed by any lawsuits.

Before using or registering a particular business name, logo, tagline, etc, (the **mark**) you should do a trademark **clearance**. This is a systematic search of various databases to determine whether others may have preexisting claims to the mark, and an opinion as to the extent to which the mark is clear of such claims.

You can do this yourself by searching Google, the website for your state's secretary of state, and the U.S. Patent and Trademark Office website, *USPTO.gov*. However, you may miss some similar marks, or you may not realize when a mark is too similar. A safer strategy is to have a lawyer do it; it generally should cost about $500-1,000 for a lawyer to do a trademark clearance search and report.

STEP 2: Protect *your* own business name, tagline, or logo from others' infringement of your trademark rights.

Within step 2, protecting your rights, there are two tiers or levels of trademark, which I like to call the (1) Basic plan, and the (2) Premium plan. Note that these are not actual legal terms, I just made this up for explanatory purposes.

1) Basic protection

Again we see the magic of the **operation of law**. You automatically get basic trademark rights as soon as you start using your branding in connection with your business (assuming nobody else was already using it). But it's not officially recorded anywhere and you don't get a certificate or anything.

The only way to confirm that you have the rights is to enforce them and have a court back you up. So, if someone else tries to use the name, you would **police** your rights by sending them a **cease and desist** letter. If they refuse, you may need to sue them for trademark infringement. If the judge says yes, you do indeed have the trademark rights, then that's how you know!

You can and should insert "TM" next to your branding, to let others know that you intend to enforce your trademark rights. The Basic plan costs essentially nothing. That is, unless you need to sue to enforce your rights, in which case it can get very expensive, at least in upfront costs.

2) Premium protection:

If you want more certainty (although nothing in life is certain except death and taxes!), a fancy certificate, and the ability to sue infringers for more money, it's time to upgrade to the Premium plan! This involves registering your branding with the U.S Patent and Trademark Office. Then you can use the nicer-looking "R" in a circle: ®. The "R" stands for *registered* trademark, and also that you are *really* serious about enforcing your trademark rights.

Registration is not easy to do, and it's not exactly cheap. This Premium plan will cost a minimum of $250 to the government, and if you use a lawyer, maybe $400-$800 in legal fees. That said, enforcing your trademark rights when you have registered with the USPTO can actually be cheaper overall, since if you win, the other party must reimburse you for your attorney fees and other legal costs.

Note that you can also register a trademark with your state's trademark registry, but this is only effective within the state's borders, so most people don't bother.

Can any name be a trademark?

Not everything qualifies as a trademark; it must be **distinctive** so that the public can associate the trademark with your business. Many people tend to want to use names that are descriptive of their services, but this is generally not trademarkable. For example, you probably can't get trademark rights for "Awesome Graphic Designs." You're just describing what the services are like. That's not sufficiently distinctive.

The best names for trademark purposes are either **arbitrary** (has nothing to do with the services) or **fanciful** (made-up word with no meaning). And yes, those *are* the actual legal terms. An example of an arbitrary name is Apple computers. A fanciful name is something like Zoox (yes that's a real company).

What should I do if someone claims I'm infringing on their trademark?

If you get a cease and desist notice, and you realize that you are in fact infringing on someone's trademark rights (oops!), you may want to get ready to make some changes ASAP. Even if under an earlier business model with limited products and services, you weren't infringing, when a business ventures into new products and services, this may encroach on preexisting brands in those spaces. This can lead to potential conflicts, and significant gray areas in determining who has the rights to what.

You may be able to work out an agreement with the other party to specify the particular products and services you each will and will not offer, and/or geographic areas you each will operate in, under the auspices of the disputed trademark. Or maybe you are entirely in the right, and want to fight them off. Do I need to even say it? Talk to a lawyer.

What should I do if someone else is using my trademark?

First of all, you need to be sure that they are in fact infringing on your trademark rights. If you attempt to enforce your rights but it turns out that you don't have the rights you thought you did, that could get awkward, fast. And you will have wasted some time and maybe money.

How could this happen? A few ways. Perhaps the name is not actually distinctive, or the supposed infringer was using the name before you did, or they are not providing the same or similar services as you do. Assuming they are in fact infringing on your rights, then it probably would be appropriate to send them a **cease and desist** letter telling them to stop using the name. If they refuse to stop, you would then need to take them to court to enforce your rights.

You may be tempted to let a "minor" infringement slide, maybe because you don't want to have to deal with it, or maybe you just want to be nice. Sounds harmless, but in fact you could end up losing your trademark rights if you do not **monitor** and **police** the uses of it. The way it works is essentially that if you aren't continually protecting your trademark, the law will assume you aren't really that interested in the trademark protection. It's kind of like if you're dating someone and you don't text them very often, they may assume you're just not that into it. But maybe you're just busy running your business!

See more about trademark at *LawSoup.org*.[4]

> "You can't use up creativity. The more you use the more you have."
>
> - Maya Angelou

8 - Use Protection: Protecting Your Work

"Is it art?" Luckily, we don't need to try to answer that thorny question. Whether you are an artist in the classical sense, or you bring your creative abilities to bear on inventions or even business plans, your work may be protectable by **copyright**, **patent**, **NDAs**, or **trade secret** law.

Protecting Tangible Work with Copyright

What is protected by copyright?

Copyright protects any original work in a variety of forms, including writings, drawings, photos, music, video, software code, architecture, fashion, business plans, etc. It can be digital or on paper.

As the creator of a work, copyright protection gives you the exclusive rights to:

1. Reproduce the work (make copies)
2. Distribute copies by sale or rental, or lending
3. Perform/display the work publicly
4. Create derivative works (works based on or derived from an original work)
5. *Music*: perform work by digital audio transmission

Keep in mind that copyright protects the specific *expression* of a work, or derivatives thereof, but not necessarily the ideas in that work. For example, you can get a copyright for a book, which means others cannot use the words of the book without your permission. But someone can take what they learned from the book and create something new from that (as long as it's sufficiently new). This is, of course, the basis of human knowledge! As Isaac Newton said, "if I have seen further it is by standing on the shoulders of Giants." Still, intellectual giants should be able to get some compensation for their work before everyone starts climbing up and standing on their shoulders. We'll discuss how to protect ideas later in this chapter.

How does copyright work?

Like trademark, there are two sides of the copyright coin: ensuring that you are not infringing on others' rights, and enforcing your own rights.

STEP 1: Don't infringe on others' work.

There's quite a bit of misinformation out there about whether and how you can use the work of others or not. Especially when much of this work is just a click away on the internet, it can be tempting to use it in some way without considering the consequences. Potentially dire consequences, that is. As in, imprisonment of up to 5 years, and a fine of up to $250,000 per work infringed!

So, you're browsing the internet, and you come across a beautiful website. Some of the graphics and photos would be perfect for your small business's website. In a few quick clicks, boom, now they are on your site. Then you use the graphics on your social media to promote your products. Done and done.

The question is: is any of that legal? NOPE. And no, simply attributing the creator of the work (such as tagging or using a hashtag) will not necessarily get you off the hook. Of course, this doesn't mean you are going straight to jail. The vast majority of infringement goes unenforced and unpunished. But again, you never know.

There are ways to tweak this scenario to make it legit. First, you could use a work *with* permission. Many photos and graphics that are online are labeled for "free" usage. There are entire databases dedicated to these free images, such as Unsplash.com.

Or you could ask the creator for permission to use it. They may ask you to compensate them for your use, or they may simply deny you altogether. If you do get permission, make sure to get it in writing (an email is fine).

Second, you *may* be able to use small portions of a work, without permission, if your use would probably not cut into the creator's potential profits. This could then be considered non-infringement based on **fair use**. Many uses of others' intellectual property is based on fair use. You know how you can google almost any book and read an excerpt of it? Google Books provides this service without getting permission from the millions of authors. Why is this allowed?

Most people who want to buy a book are not going to be satisfied with reading a few pages of a book for free. So Google is probably not reducing much profit from the authors and publishers.

Keep in mind that the fair use doctrine is a very gray area of the law, which is not well defined and changes all the time. So, you rely on the fair use doctrine at your peril. Cue the spooky music. It's always less risky to avoid using copyrighted material that you don't have permission to use.

A third way to legally "use" someone's work without their consent is to simply be "inspired" by it and create your own thing based on this inspiration. Just make sure it is different enough from the original work. Don't let inspiration become imitation!

STEP 2: Protect your own work from others' use of it.

Again, like trademark, there are also two tiers or levels of protection: (1) Basic and (2) Premium.

1) Basic protection:

Similarly to trademark's basic level, by **operation of law**, as soon as you create an original work, you instantly and automatically get the copyrights. You don't need to do anything to get this basic copyright protection, it is simply recognized by the law. It's not recorded anywhere, and you don't get a certificate. To use the protection, you just assert it, meaning if someone infringes on your copyright, you would send cease and desist letters and/or demand letters to request that they stop doing so and, if appropriate, that they pay you for their use.

When you own the copyright to a work, you essentially have full control over it. You can prevent others from using it. Or you can allow others the right to use the work in certain ways, which is called **licensing** or granting a license to use the work.

The Basic level essentially costs nothing, unless you need to enforce your rights, of course.

2) Premium protection:

You can get additional protection (potential to sue infringers for more money) if you register the work with the U.S. Copyright Office. And you get a fancy little certificate. The cost is $45 for a single work, or you can register certain multiple works together for between $55 and $95.

With the multiple-work or group registration, you can register the following:

- Unpublished works: For most works, you can register up to 10 unpublished works in a group registration, aka GRUW (group registration for unpublished works).
- Photography: You may register up to 750 photographs (published or unpublished) in one registration.
- Jewelry: You may register a jewelry collection in one registration.

- Music album: A collection of songs released together
- Published works: You may also register certain groups of published works
  - Up to 3 months of issues from the same serial publication
  - Up to 1 month of issues from the same newspaper or newsletter (regardless of whether the issues are published daily, weekly, bi-weekly, etc.)
  - A group of contributions published in periodicals
  - At least 2 and up to 50 short online literary works (A short online literary work contains 50 to 17,500 words, and is first published as part of a website or online platform, including online newspapers, blogs, social media websites, and social networking platforms. Examples of short online literary works include poems, short stories, articles, essays, columns, blog posts or entries, and social media posts.)

While you may be able to handle the registration yourself, it can also be complicated. You can hire a lawyer to handle the registration, and expect to pay them something around $200-$500.

Unlike trademark, there is no special symbol for a registered copyright. Whether registered or not, either way you should use the C in a circle © to give others notice that you intend to enforce your rights. Example: © 2022 Jessica Diaz.

How does licensing work?

Licensing is simply allowing people to use your work, hopefully in exchange for a nice payout (**licensing fees**). There are 2 types of licenses – **exclusive** and **non-exclusive**. Giving someone an exclusive license means that person is the only one who can use your work or decide whether others can use it or not (not even you can use it anymore!).

Giving someone a non-exclusive license is allowing them to use your work, while allowing yourself the ability to continue using it and to continue allowing others to use it. You can get very specific about how they are licensed to use the work, in terms of the purpose of use, how many copies, geographic scope, etc. Generally, the fewer restrictions, the higher the licensing fees.

To give someone an exclusive license, you must put it in writing (a **license agreement**) and sign it. A non-exclusive license can be granted verbally, but, of course, it's highly recommended to get it in writing.

When I create work for a client, who owns it?

When you create work for a client, if you don't have a contract or the contract doesn't say anything about intellectual property, by default you own the work and the client has only a license to use the work. You would then be able to continue using the work however you wish, or allow others to do so.

But many clients don't realize this is how it works. So, it is important to clarify the intellectual property ownership in writing. This will allow you to specify the terms of the license. If the client wants greater use of or even full ownership in the work, you should be able to charge more for that, or even get ongoing licensing fees.

Of course, not all clients will go for any of that. It all depends on how much they want to work with you. Many companies require service providers to sign a **work for hire agreement**, which automatically gives them all rights to the work. The client is then considered the original **author** (creator) of the work, not you. Or instead, they may ask you to sign an **assignment agreement**, which would preserve you as the original author, but it would transfer your rights after the fact. Either way, both of these agreements leave with you little to no rights in the work. If it's decent compensation, maybe it's worth it to you. Or maybe not.

If you hire your own independent contractors (subcontractors) to help with a client, you would probably want to use a work for hire agreement or assignment of all the intellectual property they create for the project.

How do I enforce my copyrights?

If someone is using your material without your permission, you can send them a cease and desist letter, and potentially also demand payment for their use of your work.

If that doesn't work, you may need to sue the infringer in court.

> **HOT TIP:** If you find your work infringed online, you can send a **DMCA takedown notice** to ask the website host to remove the material. DMCA stands for Digital Millennium Copyright Act, which is a law that allows for an easier way to police online infringement.

See more about copyright at *LawSoup.org*.[5]

Protecting Ideas: Patent, Trade Secrets, and NDAs

It is somewhat more challenging to protect ideas and information compared to protecting the work that contains the information. When someone simply copies and pastes a large block of text, infringement can be quite apparent. But protecting things like ideas, concepts, inventions, and product designs is murkier. Did Samsung infringe on Apple's design patents by allegedly copying the way the iPhone looks and operates? Courts went back and forth on this issue for many years, ultimately ruling in favor of Apple.

Ideas, inventions, and product designs are primarily protected through patents, trade secret law, and non-disclosure agreements (NDAs). Following is a brief overview on each of these. You can find more information on these topics at LawSoup.org.

Patent

Patents can protect certain inventions and innovations. There are three types of patents: utility, design, and plant patents. Utility patents are issued for new and useful processes, machines, articles of manufacture, or compositions of matter, or any new and useful improvement of such things. Design patents are issued for new, original, and ornamental design for an article of manufacture. Plant patents are issued to those who invent or discover and asexually reproduce any distinct and new variety of plant.

Patents are difficult and costly to obtain ($10,000+). Securing a patent requires registration with the U.S. Patent and Trademark Office, and it is highly recommended to hire a specialized patent lawyer to assist.

Trade secret

Trade secret protection is relatively easy to obtain, and there is no registration. You essentially need to clearly treat the relevant information as confidential, marking such documents clearly at the top with something like "CONFIDENTIAL: NOT TO BE SHARED." Then, if someone does "leak" or share the document, you can sue them for a violation of your trade secret rights.

NDA/confidentiality agreement

Non-disclosure agreements (NDAs), or confidentiality agreements, work similarly to trade secret, but may offer stronger protection. Before telling someone your idea or sending them a presentation about it, you may want to have them sign an NDA, in which they agree not to disclose your idea to anyone else. If the other party does spill the beans, then you can sue them for breach of contract.

> "Those are my principles, and if you don't like them… well I have others."

— Groucho Marx

9 - Working Well with Others (Contracts)

Stop me if you've heard this one before… contracts are like condoms… But seriously, as a small business, you will need to enter into contracts with various parties, including clients, vendors, subcontractors, and landlords (for leasing office, retail, or other space).

Many people are confused by, and maybe a bit afraid of, contracts. They often want to get a contractual negotiation over with as quickly as possible. But a contract doesn't need to be scary. It is simply about making sure both parties are on the same page.

It's an opportunity to make sure that you are in agreement as to what is expected, and it can help avoid issues down the road. It's much better to get things sorted ahead of time than try to hash it out when there is a dispute and things can get heated.

Getting comfortable with what's in your contract can help you have more confidence with your clients. These are your rules of the road, and you should stand by them. Assuming they are reasonable, of course.

With a contract, you get to make your own "laws" that apply between you and the other party. But those laws can't violate higher level laws. Remember the hierarchy of laws from *Law is Not for Lawyers (It's for Everyone)*? So, for example, in some states, **non-compete** agreements are generally illegal. If a contract includes a non-compete provision, that provision is unenforceable in those states.

Contracts 101

What is a contract, exactly?

A contract is simply an agreement between two or more parties that is enforceable in a court of law. This is not necessarily a formal document that says "Contract" or "Agreement" or even a document at all. You can have a "verbal agreement" (technically called an **oral agreement**) simply by speaking with someone and agreeing to something, which may also be considered a contract. A contract can even be created, or **implied** by **operation of law** based on the actions of the parties. However, contracts that are not at least written down in some form are much less likely to be enforced by a court. Even emails can be pretty good evidence of a contract; although the most enforceable contracts are a formal document signed by all parties.

These situations really depend on the specific circumstances, so definitely talk to a lawyer for help on this.

Are all contracts enforceable in court?

No. To be legally enforceable, both parties to a contract must clearly have a "meeting of the minds" in that they both were generally on the same page about the deal. Just imagine your brain and the client's brain shaking hands, if that's not too weird.

A meeting of the minds requires sufficient details to be worked out. For example, if you write an email to a supplier saying something like "I would like to buy some widgets from you," and they say something like, "Sure, I'll sell you some widgets," you probably do not have a binding contract yet. How many widgets? At what price? These are important details, without which you do not have a legally binding agreement.

Not only that, but an agreement must be an exchange of some sort, where each of the parties "gives up" something. An example is when you agree to buy supplies from someone, you are giving up some money, and the seller is giving up their supplies.

If only one of the parties agrees to do something, this is generally not enforceable. If you promise or pledge to do something, without another person also promising or pledging anything, this does not create a contract. You can't be legally bound by a **gratuitous promise**, even if in writing; there must be an exchange or bargain.

Let's say your friend promises she will give you her car when she buys a new one (Good friend to have!). She even signs a document with this promise. But you promised her nothing in return. If she changes her mind and doesn't give you the car, you're out of luck. You have no right to the car.

Certain contracts or provisions or clauses in a contract can be unenforceable for other reasons, such as that they violate certain laws. It is illegal to sell your kidney (but you can donate it, of course). If you enter into a contract to sell your kidney, that contract is unenforceable. But if you are at a point where you need to sell your kidney, you probably aren't thinking much about contracts.

If I didn't sign anything, there's no agreement, right?

No, that's not necessarily true. Contracts do not necessarily need to be signed, and as discussed above, don't even necessarily need to be in writing. It is *easier to enforce* in court if it is in writing and signed, but even if it's solely a verbal agreement, you may still have a contract that you are legally required to follow.

> **HOT TIP:** In all business dealings, be careful about the language you use and the actions you take. Don't use words of certainty, unless you are certain about the deal. Instead, say things like "that sounds interesting, but we need to discuss further" or "we may be interested in that."

Another way you can have a binding agreement is if it is **implied by operation of law**. This can happen if one of the parties starts **performing** a service, and the other party accepts that service. Say you go to a carwash, you see a sign with the price, and you allow your car to be washed. You have an **implied contract** to have your car washed for that price. No signature required.

What is a "handshake deal"?

A handshake deal usually just means an **oral agreement** (aka **verbal agreement**), which may or may not be enforceable. Shaking hands does not necessarily make the agreement any more or less enforceable, but it could potentially help to show that both sides had a "meeting of the minds."

How can a contract be modified?

Most agreements specify that it can't be modified unless in writing and signed by both parties. This effectively prevents modifications made by oral agreement. But if both parties carry out a modification, acting as if they believe the contract was actually modified, then it probably is effective.

Should I have my own contracts or let clients give me theirs?

Remember, you are the business, and you set the rules and procedures for your business. So, you should certainly have your own standard contract, customized in a way that works best for you.

That said, many clients will insist that you use their contracts. As long as the terms are acceptable to you, this should be fine. Keep in mind that this reflects their assertion of power and it could be a red flag that they may be difficult to work with.

Should I draft my own contracts or have a lawyer do it?

While you can certainly draft your own agreements, perhaps based on a template you found online, this could be problematic. The template may not be appropriate for your situation, or it may be missing important details. Each word in a contract can make a big difference, and lawyers are trained to consider these details. Hiring a lawyer to draft a custom standard contract for could potentially save you thousands of dollars in avoiding client non-payment or other issues. You can then, on your own, modify the contract for each client based on a negotiation of your client's preferences and your own.

If you find the right lawyer, you should be able to get a simple contract drafted for less than $500 total. More complicated situations may require more complex contracts that could cost $1,000 or more. Either way, it can definitely be worth the cost.

How do I enforce a contract?

If the other party to a contract is not doing what they agreed to do, or has violated the agreement in a significant way, this is called a **breach of contract**. To enforce the contract, you would start out by simply calling them out on it. No, that doesn't mean you call them and scream bloody murder. That will probably just make things worse. Instead, send a sternly worded letter explaining their breach and how they can fix it. If they don't comply, then you may want to file a lawsuit against them.

Importantly, you must be able to prove your claims to the court. In the case of a "handshake deal" or **oral agreement**, you may need to prove that there was a binding agreement in the first place (unless the other party concedes this). This can be difficult unless you have witnesses or circumstantial evidence of some kind.

To sue for relatively small amounts of money, you can use **small claims court**. The amount varies by state. In some states, small claims court is for claims of up to $5,000. In other states it can be as high as $25,000.

I signed a contract but now I need to get out of it. What are my options?

Check your contract for the termination provision. If the contract says nothing about this, then you will need to negotiate this with the other party to the contract. Or, if certain conditions apply, you may have a right to cancel the contract or otherwise be excused from any obligations. These situations include:

You may have a right to cancel or get out of a contract if one or more of the following applies:

- **Lies**: The other party **lied** about a substantial aspect of the transaction. This is legally known as **misrepresentation, fraud,** or **deceptive business practices**.

- **No True Consent:** You gave consent by **mistake** or under **extreme pressure**. The legal terms are **fraudulent inducement, undue influence,** and **duress**.
- **Extreme Unfairness:** The agreement is extremely unfair or one-sided, or the way they got you to sign the agreement was very unfair. This is legally known as the **unconscionability** doctrine.
- **Impossible:** The agreement falls through for some reason that was **not your fault**. This involves the doctrines of **impossibility** or **impracticability**.

One or more of these reasons may make the contract **voidable, rescindable, void,** or **null**, which are legal ways of saying the contract can be ripped up or unenforceable. If you are planning to rely on one or more of these reasons, you will generally need to have quite a strong case, and be able to prove your accusations.

What are the Main Types of Contracts for Small Business?

Most small businesses will enter into many contracts with clients or customers. These generally involve providing a service or a custom order of products. Agreements with clients or customers may be called a **services agreement, independent contractor agreement, custom order agreement, purchase order,** or something similar.

If you plan to have an ongoing relationship with a client, in which you will work on various projects, you may want to do a **master services agreement**. This would set out the terms that are applicable to any services you provide the client, but it would not specify those services. For each project, you would then have a **statement of work** which provides all the details about the project, particularly the deliverables and the timeframe. The master services agreement would automatically apply to each project, so you would not need to enter into a new master services agreement for each project; only a statement of work. The statements of work can be informal, and even simple emails are usually fine.

You will likely have **vendor agreements** with suppliers, detailing the products or services that you need for your business. If you hire subcontractors to help you provide your services or goods, you would need an **independent contractor agreement**.

What are Common Types of Contract Clauses for Small Business?

A contract is simply a collection of various clauses or provisions, each covering a different aspect of the agreement. Whether you are providing the goods or services, or the goods or services are being provided to you, there are common provisions which are generally found in most contracts. Whichever "side" you are on, you should try to tailor the contract in your favor. The following discusses provisions from the perspective of the service provider.

Most important clauses

Some of the most important clauses for small businesses are:

- Scope of services
- Compensation / schedule of fees
- Costs / expenses
- Intellectual Property / Ownership and Use of Work
    - Licensing agreement
    - Assignment agreement
    - Work-for-hire agreement
- Work stoppage / late fees
- Independent contractor status
- Termination

Scope of services: AKA "Don't Be a Scope Creep." One of the most important clauses is the scope of services. Make sure this clearly describes the work to be done, including timeframe, deliverables, and, if applicable, the number of revisions of the work that are included. You may also want to state what services are *not* covered, and that if the client wants extras, they must pay additional fees.

Compensation / schedule of fees: AKA "Get That Dough" clause. This one is self-explanatory, but it should clearly set out pricing, such as standard fees and fees for extra work; when invoices will be issued; when payment is due; methods of payment accepted, etc.

Costs / expenses: This clause specifies the items or types of items for which the client is responsible to pay. This may include reimbursement for printing, shipping, travel, etc.

Intellectual property: This specifies who will own the work produced under the contract. It may include a work for hire agreement, assignment agreement, and/or a licensing agreement, which we discussed in Chapter 8.

Work stoppage / late fees: This one states that if the client is late in paying fees, the service provider may charge late fees and/or stop all work until they are paid what is owed.

Independent contractor status: This declares that service provider intends to be treated as an independent contractor, and not as an employee, nor as a partner or agent of the client. It should include language that the client has no control and shall not exercise control over the means or methods of performing the services.

Termination: The "It's Not Me, It's You" clause. A termination clause sets out what happens if one or both parties want to terminate the contract and the working relationship. In particular, it's very important to specify the compensation required upon termination. It should usually be prorated based on the percentage of work you have completed. You may also want to include a **termination fee** or **cancellation fee** (colloquially referred to as a "kill fee"). This can be a flat dollar amount or a percentage of the remainder of the fees that you would have earned if the other party hadn't terminated the contract.

You should also specify the timeframe for a notice of termination. For example, if upon the client's early termination, it will take about two weeks for you to tie up loose ends, you should insist that the client must provide at least two weeks notice before the contract terminates.

Other standard clauses

Here are some other frequently used contract provisions (often referred to colloquially as **boilerplate**, as they are quite standard):

- Confidentiality / non-disclosure agreement (NDA)
- Limitation of liability
- Waiver of liability / release of liability
- Indemnification / indemnity / hold harmless
- Merger / integration / entire agreement clause
- Assignment / non-assignment
- Severability
- Survival
- Force majeure (aka "Act of God")
- Governing law
- Dispute resolution
- Arbitration
- Attorney fees
- Waiver
- Modification / amendment

Confidentiality / non-disclosure agreement (NDA): The "Can You Keep a Secret?" clause. A standard confidentiality agreement, also known as a non-disclosure agreement, simply obligates one (or both) parties to not disclose or reveal any sensitive information about the other party. It also may limit each party to using the information they learn about the other only for the purposes of carrying out the agreement.

Limitation of liability: A limitation of liability clause in a contract generally stipulates that the amount of money to be recovered in a lawsuit between the parties is limited to a certain amount (often the total amount of fees paid).

Waiver of liability / release of liability: Often used for situations involving a risk of physical harm. For example, when you sign up for a gym membership, you will almost certainly need to waive or release certain rights to sue the gym if you are harmed during your use of the gym.

Still, if the gym doesn't take proper safety measures, the member would probably retain the right to sue. (Note that this clause should not be confused with a **non-waiver** of contractual obligations, discussed below).

Indemnification / indemnity / hold harmless: To explain the concept of indemnity, it's best to start with an example. Let's say you are contracting with Maria to run an event for your company. If the contract states that Maria will **indemnify** you, this means that if you get sued by one of the attendees because of something Maria did, Maria will step in and defend you against the lawsuit, and will compensate you (hold you **harmless**) for any loss from that lawsuit.

Merger / integration / entire agreement: A merger clause, also known as an integration clause or entire agreement clause, means that the document supersedes or replaces any and all prior agreements whether written or oral/verbal, such as phone conversations or emails.

Modification / amendment: In general, just as many contracts can be made orally, even a contract that is written may also be modified or amended by oral agreement. A modification clause or amendment clause usually specifies that any change must be agreed to in writing, instead of orally.

Non-waiver: A non-waiver clause generally states that if you were to let the other party off the hook for some obligation, such as paying on time, this does not constitute a waiver of that obligation in the future, and the other party is still required to pay on time for future payments.

Assignment / non-assignment clause: A general assignment or non-assignment clause stipulates whether or not a party to the agreement can **assign** or **transfer** their contractual benefits or obligations to any other person. Note that this clause is entirely different from, and may be in addition to, an *intellectual property* assignment clause.

Severability: A severability clause states that if a court later determines that any particular provisions in the contract are unenforceable for whatever reason, the rest of the document is "severed" from those such that the enforceable parts remain in force. Don't worry, the contract won't be physically harmed in any way.

Survival: A survival clause provides that certain specified provisions of the contract will "survive" after the contract terminates. For example, if there is a confidentiality provision in the contract, the parties to the contract may want to ensure that sensitive information is kept confidential, even after the contract and relationship is terminated.

Force majeure: A force majeure clause, also known as **act of God** clause, or "shit happens" clause, provides that if something happens outside the control of the parties which delays or prevents either of them from carrying out their obligations under the contract, the obligation may be excused.

Governing law: A governing law clause stipulates which state's law the contract will be interpreted or governed under, and thus, which state's laws will apply.

Dispute resolution: A dispute resolution clause describes how a dispute may be resolved by the parties. This may include which state and county where the dispute will be resolved. It may also include a mandatory arbitration clause.

Arbitration: A binding arbitration clause or mandatory arbitration agreement generally means that if either party wants to sue the other over the contract, they must do so through the arbitration system rather than court. See more on arbitration in Chapter 13.

Attorneys fees: This provision means that if there is a dispute over the contract, the loser will pay the winner's attorney's fees. It may help prevent frivolous or baseless lawsuits.

How Contracts Work: Scenarios

Here are a couple scenarios to show how contracts can work in your favor and help protect you. Many different issues can come up in a working relationship, and it's important to anticipate these by including certain clauses in the contract. This is what lawyers do, and how they can help. But you must also take an active role in understanding and enforcing your agreements.

Scenario 1: Who owns your work?

Say you are a design firm, Designerz Co., contracting with Beveragez, Inc. to design a bottle for them. Beveragez, Inc. may want to own all the designs you create for them, and thus will likely require you to sign a *work-for-hire* agreement or *assignment* agreement. This would mean that you cannot use any part of this work for another client in the future, so you would need to keep good records to ensure you are not violating this provision.

On the other hand, if they are not as concerned about owning the bottle designs, you may be able to negotiate a *licensing* agreement. When you license out your design, you could, for example, either (1) set a base price for the client's use of the design in a certain geographic area and limit the number of years they use the design; or (2) set a higher price for worldwide use and increased length of time.

Scenario 2: Scope creep

You are contracting with Beveragez, Inc., and you have a very specific *scope of work* that sets out the details of the specifications for the bottles, when and how the designs are to be delivered, and the amount of revisions you will do. After providing the final revision of the bottles, Beveragez, Inc. says it's still not what they had in mind, and you should have known that. They need you to go in a different direction with the designs, and you haven't done enough work to deserve your fees anyway, so you need to "fix this" without additional compensation.

You would simply point to the contract and say you did everything that was agreed upon, and now they must fulfill their end of the contract, particularly the *compensation clause*. Or, if you're feeling generous and want to build goodwill, you could say OK, even though we have fully satisfied our end of the agreement, as a courtesy we will do one more revision. But, you would tell them, this does not mean you are *waiving* any of their obligations, or *modifying* the contract at all.

"If you want to go fast, go alone. If you want to go far, go together."

- African Proverb

10 – Get By with a Little Help from Your Workers

Kind of like having a baby or getting married, a major milestone in the life of a business is when it's time to hire some help. Yes, it's a big deal, but creating a workforce is manageable if you set up good practices from the beginning.

What to expect when you're expecting a new... worker? The first thing to consider is whether your worker will be an independent contractor or an employee. What's the difference? Legally speaking, there are two classifications of workers: (1) **employees**, and (2) **independent contractors** (*freelancer* is essentially the colloquial term for being classified under the law as an independent contractor).

Depending on which classification applies, there are major differences for both the employer/client and the employee/freelancer. The worker's classification can affect taxes, benefits, and legal rights, and how much control the hiring party can legally exert over the worker.

Companies, as well as many workers, often prefer an independent contractor situation rather than traditional employment for several reasons, as we will discuss. But companies do not necessarily get to decide whether a worker is an employee or an independent contractor. In fact, many employers **misclassify** (whether intentionally or not) employees as independent contractors to avoid paying certain taxes and benefits. The worker doesn't necessarily get to decide their classification either. Who does? *The law*.

That said, in certain professions and certain circumstances, it could go either way, and thus, you could structure your work situation around the law. People performing all types of activities can potentially do so as independent contractors: from designers, writers, and musicians; to caterers and personal chefs; to people consulting on business, health, life, and whatever else you can consult about; and more. For example, journalists can work project by project, which could potentially be under independent contractor status; or they can be on "staff," which would generally be under employee status.

Freelancers vs. Employees

How does the law determine who is a freelancer and who is an employee?

The employee classification is sometimes called W-2 employee or W-2 worker, based on the tax form the worker receives from the employer at the beginning of each year. It is generally the default worker status unless the worker qualifies as an independent contractor.

An independent contractor is often referred to by many different names: freelancer, gig worker, contract worker, 1099 worker (based on the tax form they receive at the beginning of each year), consultant, subcontractor, self-employed, or even boss-lady or boss-man. It doesn't matter what you call it, if the working relationship fits under the definition of an independent contractor, the worker is legally an independent contractor.

And it doesn't really matter whether the worker dabbles, or side-hustles, or is a full-time freelance; the number of hours they work doesn't really have much to do with worker classification. Except that when a worker gets closer to full-time 40 hours with a single "client," it may start to look more like an employment relationship instead.

The laws on worker classification vary by state, which can differ from the federal government, and even different agencies within the federal government! A common thread with all of these classification criteria, or **tests**, is how much the worker is acting #LikeABoss (as in, their own boss).

State law

Whether a worker is an independent contractor or employee in terms of state law varies by state. States typically use either (1) an **ABC test** or (2) a **control test**.

ABC test

California and some other states have relatively higher standards to qualify as an independent contractor. AB 5, the controversial new law that went into effect in California in January 2020, is a version of the ABC test. It states that you are an independent contractor only if:

A. you are free from control and direction by the hiring company;
B. you perform work outside the usual course of business of the hiring entity; AND
C. workers customarily and traditionally perform this work as an independently established trade, occupation or business.

There are many exceptions in this complicated law, and as of this writing it looks to be in revision. For the latest, see *LawSoup.org*.[6]

In addition to California, 3 states currently use an ABC test to determine employment classification for most employment law, including wage and hour laws: Massachusetts, New Jersey, and Vermont. Other states use the test only for some sectors (usually construction-related). More than half the states use the test for purposes of determining whether unemployment insurance applies.

In any case, a common exemption for most worker classification tests is the business to business (B2B) exemption. If the worker can show that they operate as a "true" business, with the proper paperwork, etc., they may be able to maintain independent contractor status.

Control test

Most states use a simple, less restrictive "control" type test, which asks whether or not the hiring entity has control over how the work is done, where the work is done, when the work is done, etc. If the hirer has or exerts this control, the worker is generally an employee. If not, the worker may be an independent contractor.

Federal law

In terms of how federal laws would apply, the federal Department of Labor considers someone an independent contractor based on the following factors, which include three similar to the ABC test. Note that, unlike the ABC test, not all of these must be satisfied.

Dept of Labor test:

- Extent to which you are free from control and direction by the hiring company;
- Extent to which you perform work outside the usual course of business of the hiring entity;
- Extent to which you operate as independent business;
- Your working relationship with the hiring company is not seen as permanent;
- How much you invested in facilities and equipment;
- Your opportunities for profit and loss;
- Degree of independent judgment you use in your work.
  See the U.S. Dept of Labor website for more, at *DOL.gov*.

As if it weren't complicated enough, in addition to the above, the IRS classification may vary from other laws. In certain occupations, corporate officers and service providers are considered employees, even if they qualify as independent contractors under other law.

Freelancer or employee - which is the better status?

In some circumstances you and the worker may have a "choice" of worker status. This can happen if the worker and the company agree to structure the working relationship in a certain way that legitimately meets the legal standards, as described above.

Company: Advantages/disadvantages to engaging worker as freelancer (rather than employee)

Advantages

- **More flexibility**: Companies can engage or un-engage freelancers more easily than hiring/firing employees; not as much paperwork to process.
- **Lower costs**: By some estimates, companies save 20-30% by engaging independent contractors rather than hiring employees. This is because the company does not need to pay payroll taxes or unemployment or provide other benefits for freelancers.
- **Fewer labor regulations**: Employee rights do not apply to freelancers (wage and hour laws, minimum wage, unemployment and disability benefits, etc).

Disadvantages

- **Risk of misclassification:** If you are not certain that the worker may be classified as a freelancer, you could be at risk for legal trouble due to misclassification.

- **Less control**: In general, companies cannot control how and when freelancers perform their duties, only the end result and when it is due.
- **Intellectual property rights**: If a company hires a freelancer to create any intellectual property (writing, design, etc.), by default the copyright to the work belongs to the *freelancer*, not the company. However, this is easily resolved by having the freelancer sign a work for hire agreement.

Workers: Advantages/disadvantages to working as freelancer (rather than employee)

Advantages

- **More flexibility**: The hiring company generally cannot control how or when the freelancer does their work.
- **Intellectual property rights**: Work created by a freelancer belongs to the freelancer by default.
- **Taxes**: As we discussed, a self-employed person could end up paying less in taxes than as an employee.
- **More job security (maybe):** It may sound counterintuitive, but in a way, freelancers can have even more job security than employees. When an employee loses a job, they lose what is probably their entire income. But when a freelancer has multiple clients, and loses one of them, there are others to fall back on. See "Less job security (maybe)" below for an alternative take.
- **Less onboarding paperwork**: Usually there is less upfront paperwork for freelancers to deal with than for employees.

Disadvantages

- **Almost no labor law protection**: Many laws that apply to employees don't apply to freelancers, such as wage and hour laws, unemployment and disability benefits, and even most anti-discrimination laws.
- **More overall paperwork**: Freelancers must keep track of income and expenses, and taxes overall are more complicated. Compare that to employees, who simply get a W-2 form from each employer, showing how much they were paid in the prior year.
- **Taxes**: As discussed above, taxes could be better for freelancers, or maybe not so much.
- **Less job security (maybe)**: Freelancers are generally hired only for a specific project or for a certain amount of time. As for employees, employers may be less inclined to fire them due to the amount of paperwork required, as well as an intangible sense of more permanency. Still, most employees are at-will, which means they can be fired at any time for any reason (other than discrimination or retaliation).

Hiring Freelancers: A Guide

As we have discussed, hiring a freelance worker is generally quite simple, and there are few, if any, regulations specific to freelancers (so long as they actually qualify as independent contractors under the law). The primary exception is in New York City, which enacted the Freelance Isn't Free law in 2017. This law essentially says that businesses that work with NYC-based freelancers must use a contract, and there are certain penalties for failure to fully pay the freelancer.

Procedures for hiring independent contractors

Onboarding

1. You and the freelancer should sign an independent contractor agreement
2. The freelancer should fill out a W-9 form

Ongoing

Each year, for independent contractors who you paid at least $600 during the prior year, and who are not taxed as a corporation, you must send them a 1099 by Jan 31 (and send it to the IRS by March 31). You generally do not withhold any taxes from them.

Hiring Employees: A Guide

When you are ready to hire employees (or simply can't avoid it), it's time to immerse yourself in the wide world of employment law. Because these laws vary significantly by state and locality, and change quite often, I won't give specifics here, but you can find much more at LawSoup.org. Here's a list of the major issues you should be aware of as an employer:

- Minimum wage and overtime pay
- Break periods & meal periods
- Vacation time, sick time, family leave, paid time off

- Non-discrimination and harassment
- Employee privacy, speech and social media use
- Health & safety, and workers compensation
- Interns: whether and how to use them

Procedures for hiring employees

Onboarding

1. You and the employee should sign an employment agreement, or simply describe the terms of employment in an **offer letter**
2. Provide the employee with an employee handbook describing your company policies
3. The employee should fill out a W-4 and I-9
4. Set up payroll for the employee to withhold taxes
5. Register with the state as the employer
6. Your state or local government may have additional requirements

Ongoing

1. Maintain accurate payroll records
2. Each year, you must send your employees a W-2 by Jan 31 (and send it to the IRS by March 31).

HOT TIP: Whenever you are considering engaging someone to provide ongoing services to your business, you should have onboarding documents ready to go. Particularly with small businesses and startups, things move fast, and you may lose sight of these very important procedures.

> "The best investment is in the tools of one's own trade."
>
> – Benjamin Franklin

11 - Launch Money

Many businesses don't really need much money to get started. If you have a service-based business, like consulting or designing, you generally just need a computer (which you probably already have), and maybe some basic tools and equipment. One major cost you may want to plan for is marketing and advertising. Or you may instead try to rely on as much free marketing as you can get: your network, social media, SEO, and maybe press such as local newspapers or blogs.

On the other hand, certain types of businesses will need lots of capital (money) to get going or to grow. If this is the case for you, things get a little more challenging. There's at least four different methods to get the money you need for your business: bootstrapping, loans, investors, and crowdfunding.

Bootstrapping

For many businesses, self-funding is the most feasible and desirable method of financing. The term *bootstrapping* is based on the idea of pulling yourself up by your bootstraps, a phrase that originates from the 1830s. It basically means doing things on your own, without outside help. This slow-growth method is where you put in just enough money to produce a small number of products or services. When you sell those, you then reinvest those profits into making more products or providing more services. The proceeds from these may be enough to buy advertising or better equipment, etc.

Bootstrapping can help you maintain some independence and freedom for your business, as you can avoid the pressure and legal obligations from investors or creditors.

Loans

Everyone is familiar with the concept of a loan: someone lends you money, and you promise to pay them back later, often with interest. Many small business owners attempt to get loans from family or friends, as this is often easier than getting a bank loan. Unless you have a good relationship with a bank, and a great credit score and history, it may be hard to convince a bank to give you money for a new, untested business. That said, the Small Business Administration (SBA) has programs to help small businesses get bank loans, so you may want to look into that.

If you are lucky enough to have friends or family with some extra money lying around, and they really love you, this could be your ticket. But remember: no matter how close you are to these lovely people, things can go sour when you throw business into the mix. You may think you are on the same page, when you're not even in the same book. Are you assuming it's a zero-interest loan from granny, when she really expects 10% interest?

> **HOT TIP:** Have every lender to your business, even close family and friends, sign a loan agreement or promissory note (a simplified type of loan agreement).

If you're considering applying for a business loan from a bank, there's a few things to consider. Most banks will strongly prefer that your business is structured as either an LLC or corporation. This shows you are serious about your venture. At this point you may be thinking that this sounds great for you, because if the business is unable to pay the loan back, the limited liability of the LLC/corp means that you won't have to cover it from your personal assets. But the banks are way ahead of you. As we discussed earlier, banks usually require business owners to *personally guarantee* the business loan taken out in the name of the LLC or corporation. This means if the business fails, even through no fault of your own, your assets could be on the hook to pay back the loan. Be careful what (loans) you wish for.

Equity Investment

Investment dollars may be even harder to come by, despite the billions flowing to all kinds of half-baked, clearly doomed ideas (like Juicero, the $400 machine whose sole function was to squeeze a bag of juice into a glass – we already have hands for that!). Unlike a loan where the borrower is legally obligated to pay back the money, regardless of how well or not well the business performs,

equity investment is directly tied to the success or failure of the business.

If the business makes minimal profits, the investors may lose money. Because of this increased risk, investors usually have more stringent requirements in terms of business plans, etc. They also have an ongoing say on what you should and shouldn't be doing with the business, an important consideration if you are concerned about others "watering down" your vision.

An equity investor receives **equity** (an ownership share) in the business in exchange for the money they put in. For example, if an investor gives a business $100K for 50% ownership stake, this means they are entitled to 50% of the profits. If the business has profits of $1M, the investor is entitled to 500K, making a 5X return on investment (ROI). Not bad. On the other hand, if profits are zero, the investor still gets their 50% - that is, 50% of nothing (which equals zero, in case you need help with the math!).

In terms of voting power, or how much control they may have over the decisions of the business, this is usually the same percentage as equity. Thus, if investors as a group have over 50% of the shares, they effectively have a veto power over everything you do!

Keep in mind that investors are not just fancypants venture capitalists. Essentially anyone can be an investor. Do you have any stocks or mutual funds on a stock exchange?

If so, you're an investor. If you own a share of Apple stock, you own part of Apple Inc (a very very small part).

It's essentially the same concept when you and your co-founders contribute cash (or labor) in exchange for part of the company. To be sure, there is a big difference between investing in companies traded on the stock exchange (**public** or **publicly-traded companies**) versus investing in **private companies**. When it comes to private companies, there are various regulations regarding who can invest, particularly when it comes to passive **outside investors** – those who are not actively involved in the business operations. These regulations are part of federal and state **securities laws** (a share of a company is considered a type of **security**), and they can get quite complicated. If you are considering selling shares to outside investors, you should definitely speak to a lawyer for guidance on this.

Crowdfunding

In lieu of getting a small number of large-dollar investments, you may instead consider getting a large number of small-dollar investments, or even simply pre-sales. These are both types of **crowdfunding**, usually accomplished through online platforms such as KickStarter or Indiegogo. If you go this route, be very clear with your "crowd" on what, exactly, you are offering them (and what you aren't). You don't want an angry crowd coming after you.

Similarly to Bootstrapping, crowdfunding can help you maintain some independence and freedom for your business.

"You'll never know everything about anything, especially something you love."

— Julia Child

12 - ... And Other Things Small Business Owners Should Know

Now that we've covered the big stuff, there are a few more various and sundry legal-related concerns for small businesses.

Marketing and Advertising

As you probably know, false or misleading advertising is illegal. You may not realize just how expansive this regulation is. Even if you don't intend to deceive your customers, anything in your materials that is inaccurate could be problematic. In particular, make sure you don't leave off any zeros in your pricing, as you could be forced to sell your product at a bigger bargain than you planned! The Federal Trade Commission (FTC) and state consumer agencies are responsible for enforcing these laws, and they publish detailed guides on these issues on their websites (FTC.gov).

Another issue related to marketing is that you can't use anyone's name or image in your marketing without their permission. This is because everyone, including celebrities and even "normals," has a **right of publicity**. This is also called a **right against appropriation** or **right against commercialization**. You also can't use the business name or logos of others without their permission, if it is used in a way that implies that you are associated with them at all, or in a way that disparages them. This would be considered a form of trademark infringement.

Endorsements

If a person gets paid to endorse a product or even gets free stuff in exchange for endorsing it, they must disclose this fact in their marketing or communications, such as a social media post. In general, the post must say something like "paid endorsement" or "sponsored endorsement." This issue is also enforced by the FTC.

Free Speech Isn't Free

As a small business, you should have a good understanding about free speech, **defamation**, and **false light** laws. In general, we have strong free speech rights in the U.S., with various exceptions. One exception is that it is illegal to knowingly say false things about others if it harms their reputation. And even if you say *true* things about others, it could be considered an **invasion of privacy**. Thus, you should be careful when talking about competitors, customers, or other third parties.

If you or your business are on the receiving end of some negative "free speech," this can have a significant effect on your bottom line. If someone is spreading baseless rumors that ends up hurting your business, you may want to sue them for defamation. This is also called **libel**, when in writing, or **slander**, when spoken.

Keep in mind, to qualify as defamation, the speech in question must be both factual in nature and false. Factual means something that can be proven or disproven. Opinions don't count (no matter how terrible!). As for falsity, if the statements are true, there's no defamation either. Before you go after someone for a bad Yelp review, consider whether the review meets the definition of defamation. See *LawSoup.org* for more on free speech and related issues.

Retail and Product-Related Issues

Products-based businesses, whether physical brick-and-mortar stores, or e-commerce, or both, may face some additional legal issues, including product liability, and warranties and returns issues.

Product liability

If you manufacture, distribute, or sell any type of products, you should be aware of **products liability** issues. When a product causes harm to an end-user, the manufacturer may be held primarily responsible. However, anyone along the supply chain can also be held responsible.

Product liability issues include defective products due to dangerous product design, or failure to provide adequate warning of risks of using the product (**failure to warn**). You can purchase product liability insurance to protect you against these claims.

Warranties and returns

There are federal and state regulations for certain types of products which may require you to provide a warranty or allow customers to return the product. There is also a required **warranty of merchantability** on any sale of products. This means you must guarantee to the buyer that the goods purchased conform to ordinary standards of care and that they are of at least the same average grade, quality, and value as similar goods sold under similar circumstances. Whether it is required or not, it's generally good business practice to make sure your products are good quality, and that the customer is happy with them.

> **HOT TIP:** Set clear and specific policies regarding warranties, returns, and refunds, and stick to them. And ensure that the customers are aware of these policies upfront. Place them on receipts, invoices, signs, your website, and anywhere else that makes sense.

Doing Business on the Internet

What is a terms of service and do I need it?

A **terms of service** (TOS), aka **terms of use** (TOU) policy is a contract between you and users of your website that governs the use of your website, app, or other digital product. It usually stipulates that you are not responsible for various problems the user may encounter with the website. For example, if the website doesn't work properly, or at all.

It's a good idea to have a terms of service policy to help protect yourself against claims from users that they were harmed by the website or the goods or services offered on the website. The user may agree to the terms of service by clicking an "Accept"-type button. In the alternative, agreement to the TOS may simply be implied by their continued use of the website, although this is not as strongly protective as requiring users to actively click a button.

What is a privacy policy and do I need it?

If you collect any **personally identifiable information** from users of your website (e.g. contact info or even an IP address), you are required to post a **privacy policy** that states how you will use that information.

"Success is often achieved by those who don't know that failure is inevitable."

– Coco Chanel

13 - When Things Go Wrong

Maybe you'll be lucky and have only amazing, nice clients, customers, vendors, subcontractors, etc. Sorry, but that's just wishful thinking. Even if you do everything by the book and you're super nice to everyone, chances are that at some point, something will go wrong and you may want to sue someone, or you may get sued. Studies show that somewhere between 36%-53% of small businesses are involved in at least one instance of litigation (legal dispute) in any given year.[7] Be prepared.

That's not meant to be an ominous warning. Problems and disputes are simply a fact of life. Plan for it, legally and mentally. Don't freak out. Just be Zen.

It's about operating from a position of strength and confidence. If you truly have dotted your i's and crossed your t's, then you probably don't have much to worry about. And even if you messed up somehow, and someone is PO'd, there may be a relatively simple fix. You may be able to negotiate a resolution with the other person.

Help! I Didn't Get Paid!

An unfortunately common issue in business is when you have provided goods or services to a client or customer, and they refuse to pay the full amount agreed, or worse, they don't pay anything at all. If it hasn't happened to you yet, be prepared for it, as it affects most businesses. The best preparation is prevention. Screen clients in advance and make sure they are a legitimate company with significant funds. Also, get as much money upfront as possible. 50% is usually standard. You can, of course, ask for 100% upfront; but in many industries, clients simply will not go for this.

If you do end up needing to enforce a non-payment issue, you would usually start by sending a formal **demand letter**. You would send this to the client (or have a lawyer do so), demanding the specific amount owed, and threaten to take legal action if they do not comply.

After taking this step, if you still don't get your money, it's probably time to sue. For smaller amounts owed (around $10,000 or less, depending on the state), you can take the case to small claims court, which is an easier and more informal process than a regular court proceeding. Small claims court is designed to be simple enough that non-lawyers can handle the process themselves. However, it can still be a bit tricky to navigate, and you may want to consult with a lawyer for advice and strategy.

If it's a larger amount at issue, you may be able to find a lawyer to take on your case at no upfront legal costs (although you may need to pay the court fees). The lawyer would just take a percentage (usually 20-40%) of whatever you win. When a lawyer does this, it's called working on **contingency** basis. The higher the potential payout, the more likely a lawyer will agree to this arrangement. Makes sense!

If you win the case, you may also be able to get the loser to pay your legal fees. Usually in order to get your legal fees paid, you would need to have an attorneys fee provision in your contract.

Keep in mind, even if you win your case in court, you may not ever see the money. If the client goes bankrupt or simply doesn't have the money to pay the **judgment**, you're pretty much SOL (out of luck). Because of these various challenges of suing to enforce your rights, it's best to try to prevent these problems in the first place.

Alternatives to the court

Mediation (not to be confused with meditation, which also helps with the whole Zen thing) may be a good option to start with before going straight to court. This would involve engaging the services of a **mediator** or **third-party neutral** to help reach an agreement with the other party. The mediator does not decide one way or the other, but helps the parties try to come to a binding resolution and settlement on their own.

Arbitration is a form of resolving disputes outside of court, in which an **arbitrator** (kind of like a judge) issues a binding decision on the parties. In spite of the name, the arbitration system doesn't decide disputes *arbitrarily*, although it may feel like it sometimes. An arbitrator decides who wins and loses, based on rules created by the American Arbitration Association.

Small businesses would usually want to avoid arbitration agreements, as it may preclude your ability to sue in small claims court. Arbitration is generally more favorable to larger companies as it allows them to avoid class action lawsuits, and the cases are not public record. See more at our Guide to Arbitration and other Alternative Dispute Resolution at *LawSoup.org*.[8]

Help! My Client or Customer is Suing (or Threatening to Sue) Me!

A client, let's call him Brian, came to me recently in somewhat of a panic. His client paid him $500 in advance (good job, Brian) to do some design work. Brian did what the client asked, quite well if you ask me, and yet the client wasn't happy. The client threatened to take legal action unless Brian refunded him $250. Brian was very worried about being sued. But as I told him, would this guy really sue over $250? And even if he does, he clearly has no case. Because Brian completed the work as outlined in their agreement, the client had no right to a refund. So, I told him, don't worry about it for now, and see if anything comes of it. So far, no lawsuit.

If a client or customer is suing or threatening to sue you, stay calm and think about the situation rationally. If your client has only *threatened* to sue, but hasn't yet filed anything, they may not actually intend to do so. Ignore any tough talk, and simply try to determine the likelihood that this will happen, and of any potential lawsuit's success or not. It could be a completely baseless claim against you that would get nowhere in court. Of course, the best way to know is to consult with a lawyer ASAP. On the other hand, if you know that you are at fault, you may be able to negotiate and work out a settlement so it doesn't get to court at all.

Whether you feel you are at fault or not, it is almost certainly better to avoid a lawsuit, as it could end up costing significant time and money. Another reason to avoid a lawsuit is that it will be public record for all to see.

> **HOT TIP:** Even if you know you are right, do not antagonize the person threatening you with legal action. Attempt to defuse the situation by carefully choosing your words. An apology can go a long way, but be careful not to admit fault! You may want to say something like "I'm sorry things did not work out."

If you do receive an official notice of a lawsuit against you, often called a **summons**, it still may not be a big deal. But whatever you do, don't ignore a summons! As discussed in *Law is Not for Lawyers (It's for Everyone)*, if a person being sued doesn't respond and doesn't show up to court, the court can issue a **default judgment** against them.

At the end of the day, always keep in mind that the person suing you would almost certainly prefer not to go through the whole trial and all. Unless they are crazy and irrational (which, unfortunately many people are), you may be able to avoid this with careful negotiation. Once again, a lawyer can help you with all of this.

"You are never strong enough that you don't need help."

- Cesar Chavez

14 – Helping Hands: Getting Legal and Tax Help for Small Business

Some small business owners try to DIY everything, even legal and tax tasks, to varying degrees of success. While you may be able to handle much of this on your own, I strongly recommend at least consulting with legal and tax professionals for guidance.

The basics of hiring and working with a lawyer are covered in *Law is Not for Lawyers*, so I won't repeat that here. In this section I will discuss what small business owners in particular can expect from a lawyer, including estimated costs.

Hiring Lawyers and CPAs

What exactly can a lawyer do for me?

A lawyer can advise you on the legal requirements your business must fulfill, from licenses and permits, to DBAs and more. He or she can also recommend steps to protect your business, such as contracts, LLCs, and trademarks. And a lawyer can draft and/or file these things on your behalf, ensuring they are done properly. Use the Worksheet towards the end of the book as a guide to working with a lawyer.

What types of lawyers do small businesses need?

Small businesses will mostly want to work with **business lawyers**, of course, particularly those that focus on small and medium-sized businesses. You may want to avoid "BigLaw" which are the largest law firms with thousands of lawyers. They can be extremely expensive, even up to $1,000 per hour. Smaller law firms are probably your best bet.

Business lawyers may refer to themselves as *corporate lawyers*, which generally means they do **transactional** work (paperwork) rather than getting involved in **litigation**. Those that represent clients in court proceedings are known as **litigators** or civil litigators. Some lawyers do both transactional and litigation work.

Sometimes business lawyers also handle intellectual property issues, particularly trademark and copyright; but you may need to go to an **intellectual property lawyer** for these issues. For patent-related issues, you should make sure to speak with a **patent lawyer**. When dealing with more advanced issues related to shares of your company, you may want to speak with a **securities lawyer**.

Regarding disputes with the IRS or other tax agency, you would want to discuss with a **tax lawyer**, or an **enrolled agent (EA)**, which is a non-lawyer tax advisor who is authorized to represent taxpayers before the IRS. As for help with *preparing* your taxes, you would generally not discuss this with a lawyer; instead, talk to a **CPA (certified public accountant)** or other **tax professional**, such as a **bookkeeper** who is well versed in taxes.

For employee-related issues, you can consult with an **employment lawyer**. Some employment lawyers who work exclusively with employees, and those who only work with employers. Some work with both.

What exactly can a CPA or other accounting professional do for me?

To help with your books, including accounting and taxes, you can hire a few types of professionals. Bookkeepers can help with the basics of tracking income and expenses, and some can handle taxes as well. **CPAs (certified public accountants)** have more training and skills to handle more complicated accounting (and are usually more expensive).

You should beware of a common but questionable practice by some CPAs. Sometimes CPAs offer to set up LLCs or corporations for their clients. However, they are not supposed to do this. Not only is it considered a legal violation as an **unauthorized practice of law**, but CPAs generally do not have the proper legal training, and often make mistakes when undertaking the formation of an entity. I am often in the position of fixing these mistakes for my clients. As a lawyer, even with experience in taxes, I would not prepare a tax return for a client. So, unless a CPA has a law degree, they shouldn't be handling legal tasks. OK, rant over.

Legal Costs

Legal and tax related costs you can expect to pay to set up and maintain a business vary significantly by state and city. For example, the filing fee for an LLC or corporation ranges from $50 in Arizona, New Mexico, and Mississippi, to $500 in Massachusetts. Fees lawyers charge also vary widely, so don't be shy about shopping around. In the following chart are estimated ranges for setup for both government fees and attorney fees. Keep in mind that not all of these will be applicable to your business.

Estimated Costs for Legal Tasks in Setting up a Small Business

	Government fees	Attorney fees
Business License	$0-$100	$300+
DBA	$0-$100	$300+
Seller's permit	$0-$100	$300+
LLC/corp	$50-$800	$1000-$3000+
EIN	$0	$300+
Other licenses & permits	Varies	$300+
Trademark registration	$250+	$500-$1500+

As for annual costs, these also vary widely, and may be as low as zero dollars, to several thousand. These costs can include an annual fee on an LLC or corporation (zero dollars in Arizona, New Mexico, and Mississippi, to up to $800 for California); renewals of permits or licenses; and paying a tax professional to prepare your taxes.

> **HOT TIP:** Don't hesitate to shop around and ask lawyers what their rates are. If a lawyer doesn't have the fee structure you were hoping for, find another one.

Should I use LegalZoom or other document preparation services?

It depends on your risk tolerance. LegalZoom, Rocket Lawyer, and other document preparation services help people file paperwork to create and maintain LLCs, corporations, etc. Some of them even provide lawyers you can talk to if you have questions (usually for an extra charge, of course). But if you solely rely on this instead of having a proper consultation with a lawyer, there's risks involved. These services will probably not understand your business as well as a lawyer who has taken the time to get to know how you operate. If mistakes are made due to using a doc prep service, it could be even more costly overall if you have to get a lawyer to fix things.

Recently, a client, let's call him Tim, came to me due to trouble with his business partner. The partner turned out to be lazy and crazy, so Tim wanted to force his partner out. I asked Tim to send me the LLC operating agreement, and upon reviewing it I discovered a major problem: there was no buyout provision. This should be standard in any operating agreement, as it deals with what happens when a partner leaves or is forced out.

Rather than being able to rely on a pre-negotiated buyout provision, Tim had to negotiate with his partner, who was essentially extorting him into paying over $30,000 more than he was entitled. Understandably, Tim was not happy, but he paid the amount so he could move on.

Where did my client get this problematic document? LegalZoom, of course. As a result of trying to save a few hundred dollars on the paperwork, he ended up spending tens of thousands to resolve the problems this caused.

You don't know what you don't know. And what you don't know can cost you. Ignorance is bliss... until it's not.

"Fearlessness is not only possible, it is the ultimate joy. When you touch nonfear, you are free."

— Thich Nhat Hanh

15 - What Comes Next?

It's time to pat yourself on the back. Congratulations, now you know the basics about the law for small business! Next steps are to determine your specific requirements based on (1) your city and state, and (2) your specific business activities. LawSoup.org has much of this information. You should also check your state and city government websites. And feel free to call or email these government offices, with a big caveat: although many government employees are actually quite helpful, others are not. They often have limited knowledge and even give wrong information! Use many sources and cross-check them for consistency and accuracy.

Of course, a great next step would be to talk to a local lawyer. You can fill out the Worksheet towards the end of the book, and take it to a lawyer to discuss what you need and what they can do for you.

Now is also a good time to revisit your "why" that you wrote down in the beginning of the book. Whatever your "why" entails, come back to it periodically to refresh and ensure you are on track with your goals.

I want to take this opportunity to thank you. Thank you for reading this, and for taking steps toward being a responsible, informed small business owner. The world needs more conscientious business owners like you. I also appreciate that you are adding your voice and perspective to the products or services that you are providing.

If people are buying what you are selling, this (usually) means that you are doing something right. Perhaps you are providing people with joy, or fun, or simply essentials for living life. Whatever it is, thank you for taking on all the challenges inherent in running a business, so that people can get what they want or need. Through it all, please remember to be good to others and to the environment. I wish you much success and happiness!

Acknowledgments

Thank you to everyone who helped make this book come to life, and who have otherwise made a positive impact on my life. Your help with editing, designing, feedback, and general love and support means everything to me.

Thank you to my family for sticking with me through my crazy ideas like starting a media company and writing books, and for your very helpful feedback. To my mom, Karen, for your enduring love and encouragement; to my dad, Davis, for teaching me how to write concisely; to my siblings Justin, Brittara, and Whitney, for your relentless optimism and positivity towards me; to their partners, Missy, Brad, and Matt, for your kindness and love.

Thank you to the amazing Jessica Chan, you are truly a goddess who can do *anything*, and yet you still manage to be a humble and wonderful person; to the lovely Jackie Lam for inspiring me to pursue my goals, and for your editing help; to Dave Leon for the many breakthroughs in therapy which saved my life, multiple times; to Laura Jennings; Rafi Ramirez Crohn; Isai Ramirez Crohn; Marko Budrovac; Akira Robinson; Kim Bode; Laurent Altier; Ruthie Tumambing; Roy Tumambing, Mika Yokota, Saewon Oh, and Tito Gonzalez.

Thank you to Deena and Terry of Green Pines Creative, for your generosity and efforts towards those less fortunate, and for inspiring me to do more to help others; and to all my clients for trusting me with your businesses and livelihoods. Finally, thank you to all my readers for your efforts to improve your life and the lives of others through the power of knowledge.

Legalese Translator (Glossary)

Agent: In legal terms, an agent is a representative, or any person or entity who can act on behalf of another person or entity.

Agency: An agency can refer to a talent agency, which employs agents to help people get work. It also is used as a synonym for firm, or simply a company that provides services, e.g. design agency.

Arbitration: Arbitration is a form of alternative dispute resolution (ADR), meaning, an alternative to the court system. It is a private system, but is usually a legally binding way to resolve disputes. Many companies favor arbitration over the court system, as arbitration is often much quicker and cheaper.

Articles of incorporation: The document that is filed with the government to create a corporation.

Articles of organization: The document that is filed with the government to create an LLC.

Assignment: Assigning your rights means to transfer them to someone else. This can apply to specific rights such as intellectual property, or to a contract as a whole.

Audit: As in, an audit by the IRS or other tax agency. This is when the agency requests information and documents from you to verify your claims on your tax returns. Audit may also refer to any review of books and records, such as an internal audit.

Bylaws: The internal document that sets the operating rules for a corporation.

Business license: Business license can mean many things, but usually is related to local business taxes.

C Corporation: A type of tax treatment.

Cease and desist: A letter to demand that someone stop doing something. Often you would send a cease and desist to tell someone to stop infringing on your intellectual property.

Clause: A part of a contract or law that generally refers to a specific requirement. It can consist of a few words or a few sentences.

Client: The company or individual that engages a business for its services.

Copyright: Protects any original work in a variety of forms, including writings, drawings, photos, music, video, software code, etc.

Corporation: A type of legal structure for a business, in which the owners are shareholders.

Customer: Usually used for a person who purchases a product.

Director: In a corporation, directors are the people who make the major decisions.

Disregarded entity: Simply means that the IRS does not recognize the entity for tax purposes.

Dividend: The term for when money is transferred from a corporation to its shareholders (owners).

Domicile: The location you are based, generally for tax purposes.

Employee: This term is used for a worker who is not classified as an independent contractor.

Engage: The proper term for when a client hires a business for a job or project.

General partnership: A general partnership is formed whenever two or more people work together for profit.

Gig/Job/Project: The work that a business performs for clients may be colloquially called projects, gigs, jobs, or something else. In general, the law does not distinguish between these types. It is all simply considered performing services for a client.

Independent contractor: The legal term for a freelancer, gig worker, consultant, etc.

Intellectual property: Like physical property, if you own intellectual property, you get to decide how it is used or not used. Three types: copyright, trademark, patent.

License: A license can mean several things. It can be a government requirement, such as a business license. Or it can refer to a license to use intellectual property, which grants the licensee certain rights in that work.

LLC: LLC stands for Limited Liability Company. This is a type of legal structure for a business, in which the owners are called members.

Mediation: A form of alternative dispute resolution (ADR) that provides a non-binding process for resolving disputes outside the courts.

Member: A person who owns part or all of an LLC.

Occupational license: Also known as a professional license. A requirement for many professions in many states and cities. Generally applies to doctors, lawyers, accountants, etc.

Officer: In a corporation, officers are the people who make the day-to-day decisions. E.g. CEO, CFO.

Operating agreement: The internal document that sets the operating rules for an LLC.

Operation of law: This describes a situation which is created automatically by the law. For example, when you agree to a contract, the law generally creates a legally binding agreement.

Pass-through taxation: When a business is not taxed at the entity level, but instead the income is taxed directly to the owners of the entity.

Patent: Protects inventions and designs, including new methods of doing things or new ways things work, including such various things as hand sanitizer, speed dating, and software.

Payroll tax: Taxes imposed on each paycheck, including income tax, and taxes for Medicare and Social Security.

Principal: Usually interchangeable with *client*.

S Corporation: A type of pass-through tax treatment.

Shareholder: A person who owns part or all of a corporation.

Sole proprietor/sole proprietorship: If you are the only one running the business, and you haven't formed an entity (such as an LLC or corporation), you are automatically a sole proprietorship.

Subcontractor: when a client engages an independent contractor or company for a job, that independent contractor or company sometimes engages another independent contractor (subcontractor) to do all or part of that work.

Trademark: protects your branding, including business name, logos, tag lines, slogans, unique packaging, and anything else that identifies that goods and services are coming from you.

Work for hire: A work-for-hire agreement means the person or company hiring someone to create a work of intellectual property automatically owns that IP, rather than the creator.

Zoning: Zoning refers to local laws created by cities and counties to determine how particular areas of land can be used (aka "land use"). For example, the city may decide that certain areas are for residential uses, or commercial uses, or industrial uses, etc.

Glossary of Tax Forms

1040: Personal income tax filing for individuals.

1099: Clients may be required to send this form to certain businesses and freelancers at the beginning of each year.

1120: Business income tax filing for entities taxed as a C Corporation.

1120S: Business income tax filing for entities taxed as an S Corporation.

Schedule C: The tax form for sole proprietors to report business income/loss, to be attached to the 1040.

Schedule E: The tax form for partners to report business income/loss, to be attached to the 1040.

W-2: Employers send this to employees at the beginning of each year.

W-4: Employees fill this out so employers can send them a W-2.

W-9: Certain businesses and freelancers fill this out so clients can send them a 1099.

Worksheet for Small Business

Instructions: Use this form to clarify where you are in your small business journey, and what legal tasks you still need to do. You can take it to a lawyer to discuss what they can do for you. Check ONE box from each section, unless otherwise specified.
NOTE: You can also get a PDF of this worksheet at LawSoup.org/books.

1. **Structure & Funding**

   Business Structure

   ☐ I already have a (circle one) LLC / corporation that is properly set up

   ☐ I need to set up a (circle one) LLC / corporation or make sure it is properly set up

   ☐ I want to see if it makes sense to set up a (circle one) LLC / corporation

   ☐ I am not yet ready to explore an LLC / corporation

   Social Enterprise

   ☐ I am interested in forming a social enterprise (B corp, etc)

   ☐ I am not interested in forming a social enterprise at this time

   Funding – check all that apply

   ☐ I am considering seeking investment funding and need help structuring this

   ☐ I am considering seeking loans and need help structuring this

   ☐ I am self-funding and/or I do not need help with my funding structure

2. Taxes

- ☐ I have selected the right tax treatment for me; and I have been properly filing my federal, state, and local taxes, including estimated payments
- ☐ I need to make sure I have the right tax treatment; and I need to make sure my federal, state, or local taxes are being filed properly

3. Licenses and permits

Business License/Local Tax Registration

- ☐ I have a business license / local tax registration
- ☐ I need to determine whether I need a business license / local tax registration

EIN

- ☐ I have an EIN
- ☐ I need an EIN

Seller's permit

- ☐ I have a seller's permit
- ☐ I need to get a seller's permit
- ☐ I don't need a seller's permit

Other licenses/permits

- ☐ I don't think I need any other licenses/permits
- ☐ I need to know if I need any other licenses/permits

4. Naming & Branding

DBA

- ☐ I have filed a DBA statement
- ☐ I need to file a DBA statement
- ☐ I don't need to file a DBA statement

Trademark infringement

- ☐ I have checked to ensure that I am not infringing on others' trademark rights
- ☐ I need to make sure I am not infringing on others' trademark rights

Trademark protection

- ☐ I have a trademark registration
- ☐ I am considering getting a trademark registration
- ☐ I am not yet ready to get a trademark registration

5. Your creative content & work product

Copyright infringement

- ☐ I have checked to ensure that I am not infringing on others' copyrights
- ☐ I need to make sure I am not infringing on others' copyrights

Copyright protection

- ☐ I have copyright registrations
- ☐ I will consider getting copyright registrations
- ☐ I don't need/ I am not yet ready to get copyright registrations

6. **Contracts**
    - ☐ I have appropriate contracts with my clients, vendors, and subcontractors
    - ☐ I need to get appropriate contracts for my clients, vendors, and/or subcontractors

7. **Employees**
    - ☐ I have properly onboarded my employees with payroll, state registration (if applicable), an employee handbook, etc
    - ☐ I need to properly onboard my employees with payroll, state registration (if applicable), and an employee handbook, etc

8. **Anticipating Problems**
    - ☐ I am prepared for and work to prevent potential issues such as non-payment
    - ☐ I need help preparing for and preventing potential issues, or I need help with an ongoing dispute

9. **Other Legal Issues**
    - ☐ I need help with other legal issues, related to (e.g. marketing, terms of service, etc.):

    _____

    Notes:

    _____
    _____
    _____
    _____

References

[1] U. S. Small Business Administration Table of Small Business Size Standards Matched to North American Industry Classification System Codes (2017)

[2] https://smallbusiness.chron.com/top10-irs-audit-triggers-24366.html

[3] https://www.shrm.org/resourcesandtools/hr-topics/compensation/pages/2020-fica-payroll-taxes-hit-higher-incomes.aspx

[4] https://lawsoup.org/legal-guides/trademark-business-naming-branding/

[5] https://lawsoup.org/legal-guides/copyright-protecting-creative-artistic-business-work/

[6] https://cal.lawsoup.org/legal-guides/freelancer-independent-contractor/

[7] https://www.sba.gov/sites/default/files/files/rs265tot.pdf

[8] https://lawsoup.org/legal-basics/arbitration-and-other-alternative-dispute-resolution/

www.ingramcontent.com/pod-product-compliance
Lightning Source LLC
LaVergne TN
LVHW041936070526
838199LV00051BA/2812